FINANCIAL FIRST AID

A Dollars and Sense Guide to Avoiding and Fixing Costly Money Mistakes

DOLLARS AND SENSE PUBLISHING

Disclaimer Notice:

Please note the information contained within this document is for educational and entertainment purposes only. All effort has been executed to present accurate, up to date, reliable, complete information. No warranties of any kind are declared or implied. We are not affiliated with the companies or websites mentioned. Any and all opinions expressed are our own. Readers understand that the purpose of this book is not to provide specific legal, financial, medical, or professional advice, as each person's situation is unique. The content within this book has been derived from various sources.

By reading this document, the reader agrees that under no circumstances is the author responsible for any losses, direct or indirect, that are incurred as a result of the use of the information contained within this document, including, but not limited to, errors, omissions, or inaccuracies.

TABLE OF CONTENTS

INTRODUCTION

YOUR PATH TO FINANCIAL FREEDOM

Money can be a source of empowerment, security, and opportunity but it can also become the root of stress, insecurity, and regret. The difference often comes down to the decisions we make, both big and small. Whether it's overspending on things we perhaps don't need, lending money to someone we can't afford to lose, or ignoring the importance of long-term planning, financial mistakes are easy to make and sometimes hard to undo.

The truth is though, that most money mistakes can be prevented, avoided altogether, and even those we've already made can be corrected. This book is your guide, your first aid kit if you will, to recognizing common financial pitfalls, learning from others' experiences, and gaining the tools to avoiding common money mistakes and fixing them. So whether you're just starting out, rebuilding after a setback, or simply looking for ways to improve your money and financial habits, the lessons in these pages will help you avoid the traps that often lead to financial hardship.

WHY THIS BOOK MATTERS

Unfortunately, we aren't taught financial literacy and money matters in school. Instead, we often learn about money through trial and error or by watching others make costly mistakes. From budgeting and saving to borrowing and investing, understanding how money works is a skill that can impact every aspect of our lives. Yet, far too many people find themselves overwhelmed by the complexity of financial decisions and paralyzed by fear of making the wrong move.

This book was written to change that. It's not about complicated theories or dry economic principles - it's about practical advice, relatable stories, and step-by-step solutions as well as templates to help you avoid or correct money mistakes. Think of it as a financial first aid kit, designed to help you avoid and if necessary, fix the most common mistakes that can derail your goals and dreams.

WHO IS THIS BOOK FOR?

No matter where you are in life and your financial journey, this book has something for you:

- Young Adults Starting Out: Learn how to avoid early money mistakes that can have long-lasting effects.

- Couples and Families: Discover strategies for managing shared finances and setting goals together.

- Working Professionals: Find tips to maximize your income, investments, and retirement planning.

- Those Facing Financial Challenges: Get actionable advice to recover from setbacks and rebuild your financial foundation.

- Anyone Seeking Financial Independence: Create a plan to grow your wealth and achieve long-term security by getting and keeping your finances in order.

THE MOST COMMON MONEY MISTAKES AND WHY THEY HAPPEN

We've all heard stories, or perhaps experienced them ourselves, of financial missteps that turned into nightmares. But why do these mistakes happen? Often, it's a combination of lack of knowledge, emotional decision-making, and social pressure.

Lack of Knowledge: Many people don't know what they don't know. Without the right tools or education, it's easy to overlook important details, whether it's understanding how credit scores work or knowing the long-term costs of lending or borrowing money.

Emotional Decision-Making: Money is tied to our most basic human emotions - fear, excitement, guilt, and even love. Emotional spending, impulsive decisions, and lending money to friends or family often stem from feelings rather than logic.

Social Pressure: In the age of social media, it's easier than ever to feel pressure to "keep up" with others. Fancy vacations, new cars, and designer clothes may look great in photos, but they can quickly lead to debt and regret if not planned properly.

WHY AVOIDING AND FIXING MONEY MISTAKES MATTERS

Avoiding financial mistakes isn't just about saving money - it's about gaining peace of mind, building confidence, and creating opportunities for the future. Imagine what it feels like to:

- Know you have an emergency fund to handle unexpected expenses.

- Watch your investments grow instead of losing money to scams or bad decisions.

- Feel secure in your ability to retire comfortably.

- Help your loved ones without putting your own finances at risk.

This book is here to help you make those dreams a reality. By taking proactive steps, learning from the experiences of others, and following the strategies as well as using the templates given in each chapter, you can build a financial future that's stable, secure, and free from regret.

HOW TO USE THIS BOOK

Each chapter focuses on a specific category of mistakes, making it easy to jump to the sections most relevant to you. At the end of the book, each chapter has an Appendix where you'll find easy to use worksheets, checklists, and templates to help you take action to avoid and fix common and costly money mistakes.

Whether you're reading cover to cover or diving straight into a topic that applies to your life right now, this book is designed to be your companion on the road to financial success.

LET'S GET STARTED!

Financial freedom doesn't happen overnight, but rather it happens step by step. The first step is identifying the mistakes that could hold you back, learning how to avoid them and fixing them quickly before they create financial havoc.

As you work through this book, remember that no one is perfect, and everyone makes mistakes. What matters most is how you respond. By picking up this book, being honest in recognizing yourself in the stories you'll read about others and applying the lessons in these pages, you'll be on the path to smarter decisions and a brighter financial future.

So, let's get started!

CHAPTER 1:
MONEY MINDSET MISTAKES

"Believe you can and you're halfway there"
- THEODORE ROOSEVELT

Your mindset is the foundation of your life. Life is not just about what you know but also about how you think and approach challenges. When you have deeply held beliefs like "I'm just bad with money" or "I'll never get ahead," those can quietly shape how you earn, save, spend, or they can make you avoid dealing with money altogether. Often, these thoughts operate in the background without us even realizing they are there, and they can sabotage our financial progress.

These subconscious patterns can be formed by upbringing, past mistakes, or fear and can become internal roadblocks. They lead to procrastination, poor decisions, or missed opportunities, even when you know what you "should" be doing. That's why shifting your mindset is just as important as learning the technical side of money management. How you think about money ultimately drives how you manage it.

Your mindset is like a muscle that requires strength building. Recognizing and reshaping limiting beliefs is the first step toward long-term financial growth. Mistakes from the past don't have to define your future but rather they can educate you and fuel your progress. Progress begins not with a perfect plan but with a shift in perspective.

By opening this book, you've already taken a powerful first step in that journey. You're ready to learn, grow, and face your finances head on by learning new tools. Be proud of yourself for taking this first step. Remember: All real change begins with a simple first step!

BELIEVING YOU'RE "BAD WITH MONEY"

The Situation:

Samantha grew up hearing phrases like "we're just not money people" and "finances are too complicated." As an adult, she internalized the belief that she wasn't good with money. Even when she earned a decent income, she avoided budgeting, delayed paying bills, and felt overwhelmed by financial decisions. Over time, she stayed stuck in the same patterns, not because she lacked ability but because she didn't believe she had that ability.

The Mistake:

Believing you're inherently bad with money leads to financial avoidance and low confidence. This mindset becomes a self-fulfilling prophecy, preventing you from learning, improving, or making empowered financial decisions.

The Solutions:

- **Challenge the Belief -** Recognize that money skills can be learned! No one is born with the innate ability to be "naturally good" with money.

- **Start Small** - Build momentum with simple actions like tracking expenses or setting a mini savings goal.

- **Reframe Mistakes** - See past financial missteps as learning opportunities, not personal failures.

- **Use Positive Self-Talk -** Replace "I'm bad with money" with "I'm learning to manage money better every day." Use the Limiting Beliefs to Empowering Reframe Chart in this Chapter's Appendix to learn how you can rephrase and reframe limiting beliefs with more empowering thoughts.

- **Seek Support** - Read books (you've taken the first step by picking up <u>this</u> book), contemplate taking a course, or talking to an advisor, friend or family member who you feel comfortable with and can guide you without judgment.

COMPARING YOURSELF TO OTHERS

The Situation:

Olivia often scrolled through social media and saw friends posting pictures of luxury vacations, new cars, and designer bags. Even though she was working toward becoming debt-free, she started spending more to "keep up." She booked a trip she couldn't really afford and opened a new credit card to cover the expenses. Months later, she regretted the decision. It had set her back financially and left her feeling even more insecure.

The Mistake:

Letting comparisons influence your financial decisions can lead to overspending, debt, and frustration. It disconnects you from your own goals and values and creates unnecessary pressure to match someone else's highlight reel.

The Solutions:

- **Focus on Your Own Journey -** Set clear goals based on what matters to you, not what impresses others.

- **Limit Social Media Triggers** - Unfollow or mute accounts that make you feel inadequate or pressured to spend.

- **Practice Gratitude** - Regularly reflect on what you've accomplished financially to stay grounded and motivated.

- **Make a Values-Based Budget** - Spend in ways that align with your priorities, not someone else's lifestyle.

- **Remember: Appearances Can Be Deceiving** - Many people show success outwardly, but not the debt or stress behind it.

WAITING FOR THE "PERFECT TIME"

The Situation:

Tyler kept telling himself he would start saving and investing "once things settled down." First, he waited until after he paid off his car, then until he got a raise, then until he moved into a new apartment. Years passed, and while his income grew, so did his expenses. He still hadn't taken the first step toward building some type of long-term financial security. By waiting for the perfect moment, he lost valuable time and compound growth opportunities.

The Mistake:

Believing you need ideal conditions to start managing your money can lead to years of procrastination. There will always be life events, bills, or uncertainties. Waiting for the "perfect time" often means never starting at all.

The Solutions:

- **Start Small, Start Now** - Even $10 a week into a savings or a retirement account builds momentum.

- **Embrace Progress Over Perfection** - Focus on consistent improvement, not flawless execution.

- **Break It Into Steps** - Begin with one goal and go from there.

- **Set a Short Deadline** - Give yourself 7 days to take action, no matter how small. And then every 7 days, take another step.

- **Remind Yourself: Time Is Money** - The earlier you start, the more financial freedom you'll create later.

BE OPEN TO LEARNING MORE

The Situation:

Tina felt pretty confident about her finances. She had a steady job, paid her bills on time, and had a savings account. When friends suggested she learn about investing or take a financial course, she brushed it off as that "stuff" being too complicated or unnecessary. Years later, she realized she had missed out on valuable opportunities to grow her wealth, lower her taxes, and make smarter money decisions simply because she assumed she already knew enough.

The Mistake:

Believing you "know enough" about money can close the door to better habits, smarter tools, and greater financial freedom. The financial world constantly evolves and so should your understanding of it.

The Solutions:

- **Stay Curious** - Make a habit of learning something new about money each month.

- **Take Advantage of Resources** - Podcasts, webinars, books, and online courses can expand your knowledge without breaking the bank.

- **Ask Questions** - Seek advice from professionals, mentors, or trusted peers without fear of sounding inexperienced.

- **Update Your Skills** - Technology, tax laws, and financial tools change. Staying current helps you stay ahead.

- **Admit What You Don't Know** - Growth starts with humility; the most financially successful people are lifelong learners.

STOP SHAMING YOURSELF FOR PAST MISTAKES

The Situation:

Noah often looked back on his financial choices with regret: the credit card debt he racked up in college, the job he stayed in too long, and the emergency fund he never built. He felt embarrassed and defeated, convinced he could never get ahead because he had "messed up too much." That shame kept him stuck, avoiding new opportunities out of fear that he would just repeat the past.

The Mistake:

Dwelling on past financial mistakes and carrying guilt can prevent you from taking positive steps forward. Shame keeps you focused on what went wrong instead of what you can do right now.

The Solutions:

- **Recognize That Everyone Makes Mistakes** - Financial missteps are a part of the learning process, not a personal failure.

- **Shift from Shame to Strategy** - Focus on what you can do today, not what you should have done yesterday.

- **Celebrate Progress, Not Perfection** - Every smart money move, no matter how small, is a win.

- **Use Mistakes as Lessons** - Look at your past choices as valuable data to help you make better and more informed decisions going forward.

CHAPTER 2:

BORROWING AND LENDING MISTAKES

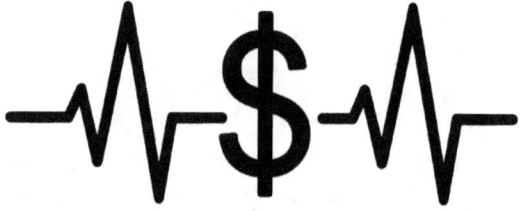

Money has a way of revealing trust, expectations, and boundaries especially when borrowing or lending is involved. Whether it's co-signing a loan for a loved one or taking out credit for something you can't truly afford, these decisions often feel helpful in the moment but can come with long-term consequences.

Many people fall into financial traps that seem minor at first but end up damaging their credit, draining their savings, or straining important relationships. From emotional decisions to vague verbal agreements, borrowing and lending mistakes are some of the most common and avoidable missteps.

In this chapter, we'll explore some common borrowing and lending mistakes and show you how to protect both your finances and your peace of mind. With a little planning, honest communication, and clear boundaries, you can steer clear of financial drama and make decisions that protect both your relationships and your wallet.

CO-SIGNING A LOAN FOR SOMEONE WITH BAD CREDIT

The Situation:

Jennifer's younger brother, Jake, had always struggled with holding down a job and managing money. Jake needed a new car but he could not secure financing due to his poor credit score. Desperate for help, he turned to Jennifer, who reluctantly agreed to co-sign the loan. At first, things seemed fine - until Jake lost his job and stopped making payments without telling Jennifer. Suddenly, Jennifer found herself responsible for the debt, with a damaged credit score, and leaving her with monthly payments she couldn't afford.

The Mistake:

Co-signing a loan means you're equally responsible for the debt. If the primary borrower fails to pay, the lender can, and will, come after you.

The Solutions:

- **Say No with Love** - Explain that your financial health must come first. Offer to help in other ways, like creating a budget or helping them find a lower-cost alternative that they can afford.

- **If You Must Co-Sign** - Ensure the loan is manageable for you in case you have to make payments, and set up alerts to monitor payments.

LENDING MONEY WITHOUT A WRITTEN PROMISSORY NOTE

The Situation:

Lisa lent her close friend, Allison, $2,000 to help with rent and bills during a rough patch. They had a verbal agreement that Allison would repay her in installments over six months. However, after a few payments, Allison stopped paying and began avoiding Lisa altogether. With no written agreement, Lisa had no legal way to recover the money and lost both her funds and her friendship.

The Mistake:

Lending money without written terms creates misunderstandings and leaves no legal recourse if repayment is neglected.

The Solutions:

- **Create a Written Agreement** - Even among friends or family, a simple promissory note can clarify repayment terms and protect relationships. Use the Promissory Note Template in this Chapter's Appendix.

- **Be Clear About Terms** - Specify the repayment schedule, interest (if any), and consequences of non-payment.

- **Use Apps or Online Tools for Payment** - Platforms like Zelle, Venmo or PayPal provide both parties the ability to track payments, which in turn can help enforce accountability.

LOANING MONEY YOU CAN'T AFFORD TO LOSE

The Situation:

David lent $25,000 to his sister to start a small business. Despite promises to pay it back within a year, the business failed, and David never saw his money again. The experience strained their relationship, to the point of even affecting others in the family, and David struggled financially and emotionally since he had emptied out his savings to help his sister.

The Mistake:

Lending money that you can't afford to lose puts your own financial stability at risk.

The Solutions:

- **Treat It as a Gift** - If you decide to help, mentally treat it as a gift rather than a loan. This reduces stress if repayment doesn't happen.

- **Only Lend Extra Funds** - Never lend money earmarked for bills, savings, or emergencies.

- **Discuss Alternatives** - Instead of lending cash, help your loved one brainstorm ways to raise funds through grants, small business loans or crowdfunding.

TAKING LOANS FOR LUXURY ITEMS

The Situation:

Jessica wanted a dream vacation but didn't have the cash to pay for it. Instead, she opened up a new credit card and even took out a small personal loan to cover flights, accommodations, and shopping. When she returned home, reality hit and she now had thousands of dollars in debt with high-interest payments.

The Mistake:

Borrowing for non-essential purchases creates unnecessary debt that can quickly spiral out of control.

The Solutions:

- **Save First, Spend Later** - Set a savings goal and pay for luxury items with cash rather than credit.

- **Use Budget-Friendly Alternatives** - Explore cost-effective travel options and deals rather than splurging if you don't have the cash on hand to do so.

- **Avoid Buy-Now-Pay-Later Plans** - These often come with hidden fees and high interest rates.

BORROWING AGAINST FUTURE INCOME

The Situation:

Nick anticipated a big year-end bonus and borrowed $10,000 to renovate his kitchen, confident he could pay it off quickly. Unfortunately, his bonus was smaller than expected, leaving him unable to pay off the loan and forced to take on additional debt.

The Mistake:

Borrowing against money you don't have yet assumes risk because future income is never guaranteed.

The Solutions:

- **Live Within Your Means** - Delay major purchases until you've saved enough to pay outright.

- **Plan for the Unexpected** - Assume bonuses or raises may be less than expected, and save a cushion before committing to large expenses.

- **Use a Sinking Fund** – A sinking fund is a dedicated savings account used to set aside money regularly for a specific future expense. Create savings categories and save the money ahead of time for planned expenses so you can pay with cash on hand when the time comes.

NOT UNDERSTANDING LOAN TERMS

The Situation:

Patrick was excited to buy his first car and quickly signed a loan agreement at the dealership. A few months later, he was surprised to find that his monthly payments had jumped due to a variable interest rate he didn't fully understand. He also learned there was a hefty penalty for early repayment - something he hadn't anticipated. What seemed like a good deal at first ended up costing him much more than expected.

The Mistake:

Signing a loan agreement without thoroughly reviewing and understanding the terms, including interest rates, repayment schedules, penalties, and fees, can lead to unexpected costs, damaged credit, and long-term financial strain.

The Solutions:

- **Read the Fine Print** - Take time to review every section of the loan agreement before signing.

- **Ask Questions** - Don't be afraid to ask the lender to explain any terms or fees that seem unclear.

- **Compare Offers** - Shop around to understand what's standard and ensure you're getting a fair deal.

- **Understand the Full Cost** - Know the total repayment amount, not just the monthly payment.

- **Get It in Writing** - Verbal promises or assumptions don't count. You are bound by the written terms.

CHAPTER 3:

SPENDING MISTAKES

You may think your money just disappears but the truth is you spent it! Spending is a natural and necessary part of life, but how you spend makes all the difference. Small, everyday habits can quietly drain your account and leave you wondering where all your money went. From impulse purchases and hidden bank fees to subscription traps and "limited-time" offers, these common spending mistakes often go unnoticed until the damage is done.

Spending problems don't usually stem from a single big purchase but rather they creep in through a series of small, repeated choices. Many people underestimate how quickly little luxuries and conveniences can add up. Awareness is the first step toward change. When you start spotting your personal spending patterns, both the helpful and the harmful, you can make more conscious decisions that align with your financial goals.

In this chapter, we'll unpack some of the most common (and costly) spending habits. You'll find relatable examples and practical strategies to help you recognize and avoid these traps and more importantly, plan around them. Smart spending isn't about being perfect but rather it's about being intentional. It's about making smarter choices with your hard-earned money. With a few thoughtful adjustments, you can reduce waste, ease financial stress, and start using your money in ways that build a stronger financial foundation.

OVERDRAFT AND HIDDEN BANK FEES

The Situation:

Carlos was trying to stay on top of his bills but often cut it close between paychecks. One morning, he noticed his account was overdrawn due to a small debit card purchase. His bank charged a $35 overdraft fee, and then another overdraft fee for a second purchase made just minutes later. When his paycheck finally hit, most of it went straight to bringing his account back to a positive amount. After reviewing his statement, Carlos realized he had been charged over $200 in fees in just one month from overdrafts, ATM usage, and low-balance penalties.

The Mistake:

Failing to track your balance and not understanding your bank's fee structure can lead to unnecessary and repeated charges that eat away at your money, derail your budget, and create a cycle of overdrafts.

The Solutions:

- **Review Your Bank's Fee Schedules** - Understand all charges, including overdraft fees, monthly maintenance fees, ATM usage fees, and minimum balance penalties.

- **Opt Out of Overdraft Protection** - While it can be a lifesaver in some situations, without it your card will be declined at point-of-sale instead of triggering a fee. And to add insult to injury, often the fee is more than the purchase!

- **Set Up Alerts** - Use mobile banking alerts or notifications to warn you when your balance is low.

- **Keep a Buffer -** Maintain a small cushion (e.g., $100) in your checking account to avoid accidental overdrafts.

- **Shop for a Better Bank** - Consider switching to a credit union or online bank with low or no-fee checking accounts.

IMPULSE BUYING

The Situation:

Helen walked into a store intending to buy a new pair of shoes for work but left with three pairs, a handbag, and a bracelet she didn't need. The sale signs and "limited time only" offers lured her in, and she justified the purchases by convincing herself they were deals she couldn't pass up. Later, she regretted the splurge when her credit card bill arrived.

The Mistake:

Impulse buying happens when emotions and clever marketing overpower logic. Small, unplanned purchases can quickly add up, derailing budgets and savings goals.

The Solutions:

- **Identify Your Impulse Spending** - Use the Impulse Spending Tracker in this Chapter's Appendix and give yourself an honest check-up of when **and why** you impulse spend.

- **Follow the 24-Hour Rule** - Wait at least 24 hours before buying non-essential items over $25. This cooling-off period often reduces impulse urges.

- **Make a Shopping List and Stick to It** - Plan purchases in advance to avoid distractions. Use the Shopping List Template in this Chapter's Appendix.

- **Unsubscribe from Marketing Emails** - Limit your exposure to sales and marketing ads that create a sense of urgency.

- **Budget Fun Money** - Allocate a small, guilt-free spending allowance for impulse buys without going overboard.

LIVING BEYOND YOUR MEANS

The Situation:

Luke earned $50,000 a year but lived as though he made $100,000. He frequently dined out, drove a luxury car, and kept up with the latest tech gadgets. To fund this lifestyle, he relied heavily on credit cards and personal loans. When an unexpected car repair drained his savings, Luke found himself buried in debt with no financial cushion.

The Mistake:

Spending more than you earn creates a dangerous cycle of debt, leaving no room for savings or emergencies.

The Solutions:

- **Track Spending Habits** - Use budgeting apps to monitor where your money goes each month.

- **Prioritize Needs Over Wants** - Focus on essentials like rent, utilities, and groceries before splurging on luxuries. Use the Monthly Budget Template in this Chapter's Appendix.

- **Cut Back on Credit Card Use** - Pay with cash or debit cards to avoid overspending.

- **Adjust Your Lifestyle** - If income decreases or debt piles up, scale back temporarily to regain control.

LIFESTYLE INFLATION

The Situation:

After getting a raise, Mia upgraded her apartment, bought designer clothes, and joined an expensive gym. While her income increased, her savings stayed stagnant because her expenses grew just as fast. When an unexpected medical bill hit, Mia realized she had no financial cushion despite her higher salary.

The Mistake:

Lifestyle inflation occurs when increased income leads to increased spending instead of saving or investing, leaving no room for long-term growth.

The Solutions:

- **Save First, Spend Later** - Automatically transfer part of each paycheck to savings before spending.

- **Avoid Comparing Yourself to Others** - Focus on your financial goals, not appearances.

- **Upgrade Strategically** - Make upgrades gradually and ensure they align with your financial plan.

- **Invest Raises and Bonuses** - Use raises to boost retirement savings or pay down debt instead of inflating your lifestyle.

UNDERESTIMATING THE TRUE COST OF HOMEOWNERSHIP

The Situation:

Melissa was thrilled to buy her first home. She budgeted carefully to afford the mortgage payment and even got pre-approved by her bank. But within the first year, she was hit with unexpected expenses: property taxes, homeowners insurance, a leaking roof, and a broken water heater. She quickly realized that owning a home costs far more than just the monthly mortgage.

The Mistake:

Focusing only on the mortgage payment while ignoring hidden or ongoing costs (taxes, insurance, maintenance, and repairs) can strain your finances and turn homeownership into a burden instead of a dream.

The Solutions:

- **Budget for More Than the Mortgage** - Factor in property taxes, homeowners' insurance, utilities, and routine maintenance when calculating affordability. Use the Homeowner Cost Breakdown Worksheet in this Chapter's Appendix.

- **Create a Home Maintenance Fund** - Set aside 1-3% of your home's value annually for repairs and upkeep.

- **Plan for Irregular Expenses** - Expect big-ticket items (roof, HVAC, appliances) to wear out over time and budget accordingly.

- **Understand Escrow and Non-Escrow Accounts** - Know whether your mortgage includes taxes and insurance, or if you'll need to pay them separately.

- **Get a Thorough Home Inspection** - Before buying, uncover any hidden issues that could lead to costly repairs later.

SUBSCRIPTION OVERLOAD

The Situation:

Mark realized he was paying for four streaming services, two music subscriptions, a meal kit delivery, and a gym membership, most of which he barely used. When he tallied it up, these subscriptions cost over $150 per month. He realized that money could be going towards paying down his debt!

The Mistake:

Subscription overload happens when small recurring charges accumulate, often unnoticed, leading to wasted money.

The Solutions:

- **Audit Your Subscriptions** - Review all recurring payments and cancel those you don't use regularly. Use the Subscription Audit Worksheet in this Chapter's Appendix to identify all of your monthly subscriptions and decide which ones must stay and which ones are simply wasteful spending.

- **Use Auto-Renewals and Free Trials Wisely** - Set calendar reminders to cancel before being charged.

- **Bundle Services** - Look for family or bundled plans to reduce costs.

- **Rotate Subscriptions** - Subscribe only when you actively use the service and rotate as needed.

NOT SHOPPING AROUND FOR BIG PURCHASES

The Situation:

Isabella bought a new refrigerator from the first store she visited, paying full price. Less than a week later, she found the same exact model at another store for $300 less. Frustrated, she vowed to research purchases better next time.

The Mistake:

Failing to compare prices and research options can lead to overpaying for major purchases.

The Solutions:

- **Do Your Homework** - Compare prices online and in stores before making big purchases.

- **Look for Discounts and Coupons** - Check for seasonal sales, promotions, or cashback offers.

- **Negotiate Prices** - Many stores are willing to match competitor prices if asked (and proven to them).

- **Time Your Purchases** - Buy big-ticket items during holiday sales or end-of-season clearances.

FALLING FOR LIMITED-TIME OFFERS

The Situation:

Sarah bought an expensive set of cookware because it was advertised as a "one-day-only" deal. She later found out the same product was regularly discounted every so often, and she didn't actually use most of the items as often as she thought she would.

The Mistake:

Limited-time offers often create a false sense of urgency, leading to impulsive spending on non-essentials.

The Solutions:

- **Pause Before Purchasing** - Ask yourself whether you truly need the item or if the deal is creating pressure.

- **Compare Prices -** Check if the item is cheaper elsewhere or has a regular discount cycle.

- **Walk Away** - If it's not essential, don't give in to time-limited deals.

GIVING CASH WITHOUT A RECEIPT

The Situation:

Marcus hired a local contractor to repair his roof. The contractor offered a "cash discount," which Marcus accepted to save money. However, a week later, the roof began leaking again, and the contractor disappeared. Without a receipt, Marcus had no proof of payment and no leverage to demand repairs.

The Mistake:

Paying in cash without documentation leaves no record of the transaction, making it difficult to resolve disputes.

The Solutions:

- **Always Ask for a Receipt** - Insist on documentation, even for informal transactions. Use the Cash Receipt Template in this Chapter's Appendix.

- **Use Digital Payments** - Pay through traceable methods like credit cards, checks, or mobile payment apps.

- **Get Written Agreements** - For services, always insist on a written contract outlining terms, warranties, and timelines.

IGNORING THE "SMALL STUFF"

The Situation:

Rachel never considered herself a big spender. She didn't splurge on luxury items or make major impulse purchases. But every day, she bought coffee on the way to work, ordered lunch instead of packing it, and frequently grabbed snacks or drinks throughout the week. At the end of the month, she was shocked to see how much these little habits were draining her bank account. She tracked her spending and saw she was spending more than $300 monthly, thousands per year, on small, inconsequential items.

The Mistake:

Dismissing small, frequent expenses as insignificant can quietly sabotage your budget. Over time, these micro-spending habits add up and limit your ability to save, invest, or reach financial goals.

The Solutions:

- **Track Every Dollar** - Use a budgeting app or spreadsheet to monitor small purchases and identify patterns.

- **Set a Daily or Weekly "Fun Money" Limit** - Give yourself a cap to enjoy small treats without overspending.

- **Make Easy Swaps** – Brew coffee at home, meal prep, or bring snacks to reduce daily spending.

- **Do a Monthly Mini-Audit** - Review your bank statements to spot and reduce "leaks" in your budget.

- **Reward Yourself Mindfully** - Plan occasional splurges that align with your budget instead of impulsive buys.

SPENDING WINDFALLS RECKLESSLY

The Situation:

After receiving a $5,000 tax refund, Adam felt like he finally had breathing room. He immediately upgraded his phone, bought a new gaming console, and booked a weekend getaway. Within a few weeks, the money was gone and so was the opportunity to pay off credit card debt, build an emergency fund, or get ahead financially. When his car needed unexpected repairs two months later, he had no cushion to fall back on.

The Mistake:

Treating windfalls (bonuses, tax refunds, or inheritances) as "fun money" instead of using them strategically can result in short-lived satisfaction and long-term regret. Without a plan, these one-time financial boosts often disappear quickly without improving your financial stability.

The Solutions:

- **Pause Before Spending -** Wait 48-72 hours before making any big purchases with unexpected money. Give yourself time to think clearly.
- **Follow the 50/30/20 Rule for Windfalls -** Allocate 50% to debt or savings, 30% to needs or goals, and 20% to guilt-free spending.
- **Prioritize Financial Goals -** Use windfalls to pay off high-interest debt, start an emergency fund, or invest in your future.
- **Automate a Portion -** Set up automatic transfers to savings or retirement before the temptation to spend kicks in.
- **Make a "Dream List" in Advance -** Before receiving any windfall, list 3-5 smart ways you would use extra money so you're ready to make intentional, and not impulsive, choices.

CHAPTER 4:

DEBT AND CREDIT MISTAKES

Debt and credit can be powerful tools or dangerous traps. When managed well, credit can help you build a strong financial reputation, access major purchases like a home or car, and even earn rewards. But when misused or misunderstood, it can lead to long-term stress, damaged credit, and financial instability. Many people fall into common traps, like relying too heavily on credit cards, ignoring student loan options, or missing payments, often without realizing the long-term consequences.

Debt doesn't have to be a life sentence. With the right knowledge and a bit of planning, you can take control, fix past mistakes, and use credit to your advantage. This chapter will break down the most frequent credit and debt pitfalls, explain why they happen, and provide straightforward solutions. You'll also hear stories that might sound a lot like your own.

By building awareness, checking in regularly with your credit report, and staying proactive, you can begin to shift the balance in your favor. Whether you're digging out of debt or just trying to avoid new traps, the tools and tips in this chapter will help you move forward with confidence and less stress.

PAYING ONLY THE MINIMUM ON CREDIT CARDS

The Situation:

Sophia racked up $5,000 on her credit card after a series of unexpected expenses. Struggling to pay off the balance, she began making only the minimum payments each month. While this seemed manageable at first, the high-interest rates caused her debt to grow faster than she could pay it down. After a few years, she realized she had paid more in interest than her original balance and still owed thousands.

The Mistake:

Paying only the minimum is easy, yes, but it prolongs debt repayment and can cost you thousands of dollars in interest, turning a small balance into a long-term financial burden.

The Solutions:

- **Pay More Than the Minimum** - Always aim to pay as much as possible above the minimum to reduce interest charges. Use the Minimum Payment Interest Calculator in this Chapter's Appendix to actually visualize how damaging - and expensive - paying the minimum only can be.

- **Prioritize Either Paying Off the Smallest Balance first or the Highest Interest Debt first -** Use the Debt Payoff Tracker in this Chapter's Appendix to list all your current debts and compare strategies like the **Snowball Method** (tackling the smallest balance first for quick wins) and the **Avalanche Method** (paying off high-interest debts first to save money over time) to pay them off.

- **Consolidate Debt** - Consider a balance transfer or debt consolidation loan to secure a lower interest rate.

- **Track Spending** - Avoid adding new charges until the balance is paid off.

NOT UNDERSTANDING STUDENT LOAN REPAYMENT OPTIONS

The Situation:

Ashley graduated with $38,000 in student loans and chose the standard 10-year repayment plan without realizing there were other options. When she lost her job temporarily, she paused her payments under deferment, assuming no harm was done. Months later, she discovered interest had accrued during the deferment, increasing her balance significantly. Worse, she had not explored income-driven repayment options that might have kept her on track without increasing her debt.

The Mistake:

Failing to understand student loan repayment options, deferment pitfalls, and interest accrual rules can result in higher balances, longer repayment periods, and unnecessary financial stress.

The Solutions:

- **Know Your Options** - Learn about all federal repayment plans, including income-driven repayment (IDR), graduated, and extended plans to find the best fit for your financial situation.

- **Understand Deferment vs. Forbearance** - Both pause payments, but interest may still accumulate. Always check whether your loan type is subsidized (interest-free during deferment) or unsubsidized.

- **Use Loan Simulators -** Federal Student Aid's Loan Simulator (studentaid.gov) can show how different plans affect total repayment and monthly payments.

- **Contact Your Servicer Regularly** - Ask questions, update income information, and recertify your repayment plan on time to avoid default.

- **Avoid "Set It and Forget It" Thinking** - Revisit your plan annually or after any major life or income change to ensure it still aligns with your budget.

TAKING PAYDAY LOANS

The Situation:

Josh needed $500 to cover rent after his car broke down. With no emergency fund, he turned to a payday loan service. He borrowed the money but quickly found himself stuck paying back fees and interest rates that exceeded 400% APR. Each renewal of the loan dug him deeper into debt, and it took him months to break free.

The Mistake:

Payday loans often come with astronomical interest rates and fees, trapping borrowers in cycles of debt that are hard to escape.

The Solutions:

- **Build an Emergency Fund -** Set aside small amounts regularly to avoid borrowing in emergencies.

- **Explore Alternatives** - Look into personal loans, credit union loans, or borrowing from family or friends.

- **Negotiate Payment Plans** - Work directly with creditors to arrange manageable payment schedules.

- **Seek Financial Counseling** - Nonprofit credit counselors can help create a repayment plan and negotiate better terms.

IGNORING CREDIT REPORTS

The Situation:

Emma applied for a mortgage and was shocked when she was denied due to a low credit score. Upon reviewing her credit report, she discovered several errors, including accounts that didn't belong to her. Because she had never checked her credit report, these errors had gone unnoticed for years, damaging her creditworthiness.

The Mistake:

Failing to monitor credit reports can lead to overlooked errors, fraud, or identity theft that damages your credit score and borrowing ability.

The Solutions:

- **Check Reports Regularly** - Review your credit reports from the three major bureaus (Experian, Equifax, and TransUnion) at least once a year at AnnualCreditReport.com - the ONLY website authorized by the Federal Government to provide you with a Free Credit Report. Use the Credit Report Review Checklist in this Chapter's Appendix to make sure you order your free reports and review them thoroughly.

- **Dispute Errors Immediately** - Report inaccuracies and follow up to ensure they're corrected.

- **Monitor Your Credit Score** - Use free credit monitoring tools to track changes and spot problems early. Many banks offer this as a free service through their mobile apps.

- **Set Fraud Alerts** - If you suspect identity theft, notify credit bureaus to flag your account.

OVER-RELIANCE ON CREDIT CARDS

The Situation:

After losing his job, Matthew began using credit cards to cover groceries, utilities, and other daily expenses. While he expected to pay it off once he found new work, months passed, and his balances grew out of control. Even after getting a new job, he struggled to dig out from the debt he accumulated.

The Mistake:

Using credit cards to fund basic living expenses often leads to unsustainable debt and financial insecurity.

The Solutions:

- **Create a Realistic Budget** - Focus on building a budget that prioritizes necessities and cuts unnecessary expenses.

- **Build a Cash Reserve** - Work toward a savings buffer to cover emergencies and prevent reliance on credit.

- **Switch to Debit or Cash -** Use debit cards or cash for daily expenses to avoid adding to credit balances.

- **Seek Professional Help** - Financial counselors can help with budgeting strategies and debt management plans.

OPENING TOO MANY CREDIT CARDS

The Situation:

Charlotte opened multiple credit cards to take advantage of rewards and sign-up bonuses. While she enjoyed free flights and cashback, juggling multiple payments became overwhelming. She missed a payment on one card, which lowered her credit score, and the high balances hurt her debt-to-income ratio.

The Mistake:

Opening too many credit cards can lead to overspending, missed payments, and a lower credit score due to hard inquiries and high utilization rates.

The Solutions:

- **Limit New Accounts -** Only open new credit lines when absolutely necessary.

- **Focus on a Few Cards** - Use one or two cards with favorable terms and rewards that match your spending habits (mileage, cash back).

- **Automate Payments** - Set up automatic payments to avoid late fees and missed deadlines.

- **Monitor Utilization Rates** - Keep your credit utilization below 30% of your total limit to maintain a healthy score.

MISSING DUE DATES

The Situation:

Jason had a lot on his plate. Between work, family, and side projects, managing his finances fell to the bottom of his list. He often forgot to make his credit card payments on time, not because he didn't have the money, but because the due dates slipped his mind. Over time, late fees added up, his credit score took a hit, and he even lost access to a promotional 0% APR offer.

The Mistake:

Failing to make credit card payments on time can result in costly late fees, penalty interest rates, and long-term damage to your credit score.

The Solutions:

- **Set Payment Reminders** - Use your phone calendar or banking app to alert you before the due date.

- **Automate Minimum Payments** - Schedule automatic payments for at least the minimum to protect your credit.

- **Consolidate Due Dates** - Call your credit card issuers to request aligning due dates for easier management. Some credit card issuers will allow you to pick your due date. If that's the case, pick a date right after a steady direct deposit, like your paycheck, to be sure there is money in your account.

- **Use a Spreadsheet -** Keep a visual tracker or spreadsheet to monitor all upcoming payments in one place. Use the Due Date Calendar Template in this Chapter's Appendix.

CHAPTER 5:
SAVINGS AND INVESTING MISTAKES

Saving and investing are good habits and they are essential to building long-term financial security. But even well-meaning people can make simple missteps that hold them back from reaching their goals. Whether it's delaying retirement contributions, skipping the emergency fund, or reacting emotionally to market swings, these mistakes can erode your progress. Fortunately, most of them are preventable once you know what to look out for.

Many of the most damaging errors come not from lack of effort, but from lack of information or planning. People often underestimate how powerful small, consistent actions can be especially when it comes to compound growth, employer matches, and diversification. Other times, fear or confusion leads to inaction, leaving money sitting idle in a checking account instead of working for your future. But it's never too late to adjust course.

In this chapter, we'll walk through the most common savings and investing mistakes and show you how to avoid them. You'll get practical advice for creating better habits, maximizing your resources, and building a plan that fits your real life. With the right mindset and tools, you can make your money work smarter and protect yourself from future financial setbacks.

KEEPING ALL SAVINGS IN A CHECKING ACCOUNT

The Situation:

Danielle was proud of herself for building up a savings cushion, but she kept the entire amount in her regular checking account for easy access. Over time, she found herself dipping into the money for non-essentials such as a new phone, last-minute weekend trips, and extra takeout. By the end of the year, her savings had shrunk significantly, and she'd earned zero interest on what remained.

The Mistake:

Storing all your savings in a checking account makes it too easy to spend and causes you to miss out on potential interest earnings that could help your money grow passively.

The Solutions:

- **Use a High-Yield Savings Account** - Earn more interest while keeping your savings safe and separate.

- **Create Digital Distance** - Move your savings to a separate bank or account that's not connected to your debit card.

- **Automate Transfers -** Schedule regular deposits into your savings account so it grows without effort.

- **Label Your Savings** - Give each account a name like "Emergency Fund" or "Vacation Fund" to reinforce its purpose.

- **Set Limits on Transfers** - Many savings accounts restrict frequent withdrawals, which can reduce impulse spending.

NOT BUILDING AN EMERGENCY FUND

The Situation:

Violet was living paycheck to paycheck when her car broke down. Without an emergency fund, she had to put the $1,200 repair bill on her credit card, which she couldn't pay off right away. The interest piled up, and what started as a minor inconvenience turned into a long-term financial burden.

The Mistake:

Failing to set aside money for emergencies leaves you vulnerable to debt and financial stress when unexpected expenses arise.

The Solutions:

- **Start Small** - Set aside $500–$1,000 as a starter emergency fund and gradually build it to cover 3–6 months of expenses. Use the Emergency Fund Builder in this Chapter's Appendix to determine the amount you should have in an Emergency Fund.

- **Automate Savings** - Use automatic transfers to a separate savings account to make saving consistent.

- **Keep It Accessible** - Store emergency funds in a high-yield savings account for easy access and growth.

- **Replenish After Use** - If you dip into the fund, make it a priority to rebuild it quickly.

DELAYING RETIREMENT SAVINGS

The Situation:

James was in his 40s when he finally started thinking about retirement. He had always believed he had plenty of time to save later. By the time he began contributing to his 401(k), he had missed out on over a decade of compound growth. Now, he's playing catch-up and contributing more than he can comfortably afford to make up for lost time.

The Mistake:

Procrastinating on retirement savings means losing out on compound interest, making it harder to reach financial goals later in life.

The Solutions:

- **Start Early** - Even small contributions in your 20s can grow significantly over time due to compound interest.

- **Use Employer Plans** - Enroll in 401(k) plans or IRAs as soon as possible and increase contributions as your income grows.

- **Automate Contributions** - Make saving easier by setting up automatic payroll deductions.

- **Increase Contributions Over Time** - Adjust contributions upward as your salary increases.

CASHING OUT RETIREMENT ACCOUNTS EARLY

The Situation:

When Ava lost her job, she panicked and cashed out her 401(k) to cover bills. She faced a 10% penalty, paid taxes on the withdrawal, and sacrificed years of future growth. Later, when she found a new job, she realized how much harder retirement planning had become.

The Mistake:

Cashing out retirement accounts early leads to penalties, taxes, and lost growth potential, making long-term financial security harder to achieve.

The Solutions:

- **Consider Alternatives First -** Use emergency savings or side gigs before tapping retirement funds.

- **Take a Loan Instead** - If absolutely necessary, some plans allow loans without penalties (but pay them back quickly).

- **Roll Over Funds** - Transfer balances into an IRA or your new employer's plan to keep retirement savings intact.

- **Create a Backup Plan -** Build a stronger emergency fund to reduce the temptation to dip into retirement savings.

LETTING EMOTIONS DRIVE INVESTING DECISIONS

The Situation:

During a market upswing, Jordan felt pressure to jump on the latest "hot stock" after seeing social media posts about friends making big returns. He invested a large chunk of his savings without fully researching the company. A few weeks later, the stock tanked after disappointing earnings, and Jordan panicked and sold his shares, at a loss. Months later, the same stock recovered, but Jordan had already moved his money into another risky pick that also underperformed. His emotional reactions cost him thousands.

The Mistake:

Making investment decisions based on fear, hype, or social pressure, rather than research and long-term planning, can lead to buying high, selling low, and missing out on steady gains. Emotional investing often results in costly, reactionary moves that derail financial goals.

The Solutions:

- **Have a Plan -** Build an investment strategy based on your goals, timeline, and risk tolerance and stick to it.

- **Avoid Timing the Market -** It is nearly impossible to predict highs and lows. Focus on long-term growth instead.

- **Stay Calm During Volatility** - Don't panic-sell when the market dips. Remember that short-term losses are part of investing.

- **Limit Outside Noise -** Turn down social media, TV pundits, and hot tips that encourage emotional investment decision-making.

- **Automate Your Investing -** Use dollar-cost averaging to invest a set amount regularly, which removes emotion from the process. Dollar-cost averaging means putting the same amount of money into an investment regularly, like every week or every month. This helps reduce the impact of market volatility and lowers risk because you buy some shares when prices are high and more when prices are low.

INVESTING WITHOUT RESEARCH

The Situation:

Brian heard about a "hot stock" from a friend and invested $5,000 without doing any research. The company soon filed for bankruptcy, and Brian lost all his money. He later realized he had put blind faith in a tip without understanding the risks involved.

The Mistake:

Investing based on tips, trends, or hype without research can lead to losses.

The Solutions:

- **Do Your Homework** - Study company financials, industry trends, and risk factors before investing.

- **Consult Experts** - Work with financial advisors or use reputable resources for guidance.

- **Avoid Get-Rich-Quick Schemes** - Be skeptical of investments promising unusually high returns.

- **Test with Small Amounts -** Start with small investments to test strategies before committing larger sums.

FAILING TO DIVERSIFY INVESTMENTS

The Situation:

Ian was excited about a hot new tech company and decided to invest nearly all his savings into its stock. At first, the value climbed quickly, and he felt like a financial genius. But when the market took a downturn and the company faced unexpected challenges, the stock plummeted. Without other investments to balance the loss, Ian's portfolio took a major hit, as did his confidence.

The Mistake:

Putting all your money into a single investment, a single stock or sector, or a single real estate deal exposes you to unnecessary risk. If that one investment performs poorly, your entire financial future could suffer.

The Solutions:

- **Spread Your Investments** - Allocate investment funds across different asset classes like stocks, bonds, mutual funds, and real estate to reduce your risk.

- **Avoid Putting "All Your Eggs in One Basket"** - Don't let any single investment dominate your portfolio.

- **Use Index Funds -** Low-cost index funds provide instant diversification, meaning lower risk with broad market exposure.

- **Rebalance Regularly -** Adjust your portfolio to maintain a healthy mix as markets fluctuate and as your risk tolerance and goals change.

- **Invest for the Long Term** - Focus on a strategy that grows steadily over time instead of chasing short-term gains.

- **Seek Professional Advice** - Financial planners can help create a diversified strategy based on your goals.

NOT TAKING ADVANTAGE OF EMPLOYER MATCHES

The Situation:

Leo's employer offered a 5% 401(k) match. Leo was only contributing 2%, because he wanted more in his take home net pay. Therefore, his employer was only matching 2% for him. Over the years, Leo missed out on thousands of dollars in free money that could have more than doubled his contributions and boosted his retirement savings.

The Mistake:

Failing to maximize employer matching contributions is like leaving free money on the table.

The Solutions:

- **Contribute Enough to Maximize Matches** - Prioritize meeting the match amount to take full advantage of employer contributions.

- **Increase Gradually** - If contributing the full match isn't feasible right away, increase by 1% annually until you reach the match limit.

- **View It as Free Money** - Treat employer matches as part of your compensation package and don't leave it unused.

CHAPTER 6:
TAX AND LEGAL MISTAKES

Taxes and legal matters might not be the flashiest parts of your financial life, but neglecting them can have serious - and expensive - consequences. Late tax filings, missed deductions, or the lack of an estate plan might seem like small oversights, but they can snowball into major problems. Many people avoid these topics because they feel intimidating or dull, but a little proactive planning goes a long way.

From freelancers not making estimated tax payments to families without a basic estate plan, these issues do not stem from bad intentions but often, from a lack of knowledge or preparation. Unfortunately, the cost of ignoring them can be steep: IRS penalties, unnecessary legal battles, or leaving loved ones unprotected in times of crisis. Most of these mistakes are completely preventable with a bit of guidance and planning.

In this chapter, we'll highlight the most common tax and legal missteps and offer simple, realistic strategies to help you avoid them. You'll learn how to stay organized, make informed decisions, and use professional help when needed. With the right tools and mindset, you can protect what you've built, reduce stress, and make sure your finances and your wishes are in order.

NOT FILING TAXES ON TIME

The Situation:

Daniel had a busy year and kept putting off filing his taxes. When he finally got around to it months later, he faced penalties and interest charges that added hundreds of dollars to his tax bill.

The Mistake:

Failing to file taxes on time results in penalties, interest charges, and potential legal trouble if ignored entirely. Furthermore, if you don't file your tax return within three years of the original due date, you forfeit your right to claim any refund and leave it in the IRS' or your state's coffers.

The Solutions:

- **Set Reminders** - Mark tax deadlines on your calendar or set alerts in your phone to stay on track. File as soon as you have all of your necessary tax documents, even if you know you'll owe. Use the Tax Document Checklist in this Chapter's Appendix as a guide to gather everything you need before filing and avoid missing important forms.

- **File an Extension** - If you can't file by the deadline, request an extension to avoid late-filing penalties. Keep in mind that filing an extension is only an extension for the filing of the tax return, not for the tax due. Therefore, interest charges accrue on your tax balance.

- **Pay What You Can** - Even if you can't pay the full amount owed, pay as much as possible to reduce interest charges.

- **Hire a Professional** - Simplify the process by working with a tax preparer or an accountant who can guide you accordingly. Ask friends and family for recommendations and check the tax professional's web presence and online reviews.

OVERLOOKING TAX DEDUCTIONS OR CREDITS

The Situation:

John paid for work-related travel and educational expenses as well as made some charitable contributions throughout the year but didn't realize he could deduct them. After talking to a tax advisor the following year, he discovered he had missed out on hundreds of dollars in potential tax savings.

The Mistake:

Many people fail to take advantage of deductions and credits because they aren't aware of if and how they qualify.

The Solutions:

- **Research Eligibility** - Review IRS guidelines or consult a tax professional to identify deductions for education, home office expenses, charitable contributions, and more.

- **Keep Receipts** - Maintain receipts for deductible expenses throughout the year to make filing easier. Use the Charitable Contributions Log in this Chapter's Appendix to log charitable contributions throughout the year. You can also customize it to log work related and other deductible expenses. This is simply an organizational tool for you. You'll still need the supporting receipts as well.

- **Use Tax Software** - Programs like TurboTax can help you identify deductions and credits you may have missed but can only be helpful if you know to look for them. Remember, using these do-it-yourself programs are only as good as the information you enter into them.

- **Hire a Professional** - Simplify the process by working with a tax preparer or an accountant who can guide you accordingly. Ask friends and family for recommendations and check the tax professional's web presence and online reviews.

FAILING TO KEEP TAX RECORDS

The Situation:

Natalie was audited by the IRS and couldn't find the receipts for several major deductions she claimed. As a result of the audit, when she couldn't produce the documentation, the deductions were not allowed and she had to pay the tax due plus interest and penalties.

The Mistake:

Not keeping proper records can lead to trouble during audits or when verifying past returns.

The Solutions:

- **Create a Filing System** - Organize receipts, tax forms, and bank statements in folders, either physically or digitally. Physically could be as simple as a shoebox where you just throw in your receipts – just in case!

- **Keep Records for At Least 7 Years** - Hold onto tax returns and supporting documents in case of audits.

- **Scan and Save Digitally** - Use apps or scanners to store receipts and documents electronically for added security.

- **Use Accounting Software** - Tools like QuickBooks or Mint can streamline record-keeping.

NOT PAYING ESTIMATED TAXES AS A FREELANCER

The Situation:

William left his full-time job to start a freelance graphic design business. He loved the freedom and flexibility, but when tax season arrived, he was shocked to find out he owed thousands of dollars, plus penalties for not making estimated payments throughout the year. Without taxes being automatically withheld like they were at his old job, he had not realized he needed to pay quarterly, or at the very least plan ahead, and now he was playing catch-up with the IRS.

The Mistake:

Failing to pay estimated taxes as a self-employed individual or freelancer can result in underpayment penalties, interest charges, and a large, unexpected tax bill at year's end.

The Solutions:

- **Know the Rules** - If you expect to owe $1,000 or more in taxes for the year, the IRS requires quarterly estimated payments.

- **Set Aside a Percentage** - Reserve 25-30% of your freelance income for taxes to stay ahead.

- **Use IRS Form 1040-ES** - This form helps you calculate and submit quarterly tax payments on time.

- **Work with a Pro** - A tax advisor can help you estimate properly and take advantage of deductions.

- **Automate Your Payments** - Set calendar reminders or use IRS Direct Pay to avoid missed deadlines.

NOT HAVING A WILL OR ESTATE PLAN

The Situation:

When Lydia's father passed away unexpectedly, he didn't have a will. The family spent months in court trying to settle his estate, and disagreements over assets caused tension among Lydia and her siblings as well as other relatives. Much of his wealth was tied up in legal fees and delays.

The Mistake:

Failing to create a will or estate plan leaves loved ones unprepared and can lead to disputes, delays, and unnecessary costs.

The Solutions:

- **Draft a Will** - Specify how you want your assets distributed and name guardians for dependents.

- **Review and Update Regularly** - Update your will after major life changes like marriage, divorce, or the birth of a child.

- **Consider a Trust** - For larger estates, trusts can help avoid probate and provide additional protection.

- **Consult an Estate Planning Attorney** - Work with an attorney to ensure your plan covers all legal requirements. Use the Will & Estate Organizer in this Chapter's Appendix as a starting point to gather and list your important information so that you can review it thoroughly with an attorney.

IGNORING POWER OF ATTORNEY NEEDS

The Situation:

When Dylan was hospitalized and comatose after a car accident, his family struggled to make medical and financial decisions on his behalf because he had not designated a power of attorney. Important bills went unpaid, and disagreements arose about his medical care.

The Mistake:

Not appointing someone to handle finances or medical decisions in an emergency can lead to confusion and delays.

The Solutions:

- **Set Up a Financial Power of Attorney (POA) -** Designate someone you trust to handle bills, taxes, and other financial matters if you're unable to. Use the Power of Attorney Authorization Template in this Chapter's Appendix as a starting point. Consult an attorney in your state to properly complete and validate any legal POA forms.

- **Create a Healthcare Directive -** Specify your medical preferences and assign a healthcare proxy to make decisions for you. See the Health Care Proxy Template in this Chapter's Appendix. Review it with a legal or medical professional to ensure the form complies with your state's requirements.

- **Review Regularly** - Update documents as relationships and circumstances change.

- **Inform Trusted Individuals** - Be sure to let the people you've named in these documents know in advance and make sure they know where to find them if there's ever an emergency. You may even want to consider giving them their own copy for safekeeping and easier access.

NOT PROTECTING WHAT YOU ALREADY HAVE

The Situation:

Angela worked hard to furnish her apartment with quality furniture, electronics, and personal belongings over the years. One night, a neighbor's kitchen fire spread to her unit, destroying nearly everything she owned. She didn't have renters insurance and assumed her landlord's policy would cover her losses. She was shocked to find out it didn't. Her landlord's policy covers the damage to the building itself but not Angela's possessions. Angela had to replace everything out of pocket, and it took years to financially recover.

The Mistake:

Focusing only on income and savings while ignoring asset protection can be financially devastating. Without renters, homeowners, or umbrella insurance, one unexpected event - a fire, theft, lawsuit, or accident - can wipe out years of progress in minutes.

The Solutions:

- **Get the Right Coverage** - If you rent, purchase renters insurance. If you own a home, make sure your homeowners policy covers both structure and contents adequately.

- **Understand What's Covered** - Review policy limits, exclusions, and deductible amounts to avoid unpleasant surprises during a claim.

- **Create an Inventory** - Use photos, videos, and receipts to document valuable items. This speeds up claims and ensures fair reimbursement. Use the Home Inventory Worksheet in this Chapter's Appendix.

- **Consider Umbrella Insurance** - A low-cost umbrella policy can provide extra liability protection beyond your home and auto insurance, and is especially useful if you have assets to protect.

- **Review Annually** - Update your coverage as your property value or lifestyle changes (e.g., buying new electronics, jewelry, or renovating your home).

NOT NAMING A CONTINGENT BENEFICIARY ON A LIFE INSURANCE POLICY

The Situation:

Hailey purchased a life insurance policy to protect her young daughter. She named her sister as the primary beneficiary, confident her daughter would be well cared for so she didn't bother naming a contingent (or secondary) beneficiary. If her sister unexpectedly passed away, with no contingent beneficiary listed, and then something had happened to Hailey, the life insurance proceeds would have gone to Hailey's estate, potentially delaying access to the funds and creating unnecessary complications.

The Mistake:

Failing to name a contingent (secondary) beneficiary means if the primary beneficiary is unable to receive the benefit, the payout may go to your estate leading to delays, probate, and unintended distributions. One of the greatest advantages of a life insurance policy is the money goes directly to the named beneficiary (primary and if the primary has pre-deceased you, secondary) and avoids probate court.

The Solutions:

- **Always Name a Contingent -** Designate at least one backup beneficiary when setting up your policy.

- **Review Annually** - Revisit your beneficiary designations each year or after major life changes.

- **Be Specific -** Include full names, relationships, and contact information to avoid confusion.

- **Update Promptly** - If a beneficiary passes away or your life circumstances change, update your policy right away.

SIGNING A LEASE WITHOUT UNDERSTANDING THE COMMITMENT

The Situation:

Nicole found an apartment she liked and, feeling pressured by the rental market and the landlord showing the apartment, she signed the lease and paid the deposit on the spot. A few days later, she found a better place with more space and lower rent. She called the first landlord to back out and ask for her deposit back. She was shocked when he told her the lease was binding and the deposit was nonrefundable. Nicole hadn't realized that by signing, she was legally committing to the apartment even before move-in.

The Mistake:

Signing a lease or rental agreement before fully understanding the terms, including refund policies and cancellation penalties, can lead to lost deposits, legal obligations, and unnecessary stress, even if you change your mind before moving in.

The Solutions:

- **Slow Down and Read Carefully** - Never sign a lease (or anything else for that matter) under pressure. Ask for a day or two to review it privately before committing by signing. Review all of the terms carefully and never assume anything that is not written in the contract is guaranteed.

- **Ask About Refund Policies** - Clarify whether the deposit is refundable if you cancel, and under what conditions. Get it in writing.

- **Don't Sign Until You're Sure** - Touring multiple properties and comparing terms can help avoid rushed decisions.

- **Understand What You're Signing** - A lease is a legal contract. Once signed, you may be liable for rent, even if you haven't moved in.

- **Negotiate Before Signing** - If you have concerns (like needing flexibility), ask the landlord to modify or clarify the lease before agreeing.

CHAPTER 7:
WORK AND CAREER MISTAKES

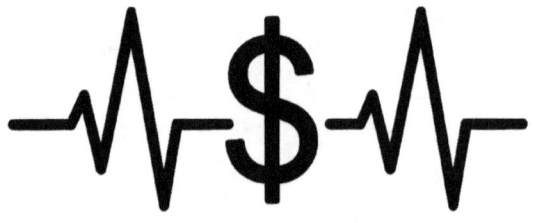

The biggest mistake people make is viewing their job or career as just a source of income. In truth, it's one of your most valuable financial assets. The decisions and choices you make at work and in your career path can significantly impact your income, stability, and future opportunities. From salary negotiations to professional development, the way you manage your career plays a major role in your financial future. But too often, people make avoidable mistakes that limit their earning potential, damage their reputation, or leave them unprepared for change. Many people miss out on potential income and career growth simply because they don't ask, don't plan, or don't prepare for the unexpected.

Whether it's quitting without notice, avoiding negotiations, or ignoring opportunities to grow, career missteps can have lasting consequences. Some mistakes may stem from fear, others from burnout, or simply not knowing better. And in today's economy, failing to plan for job loss or overlooking benefits can make an already stressful situation much worse. These are all areas where a little awareness and action can make a huge difference.

In this chapter, we'll break down common work and career pitfalls and give you practical, real-world strategies to avoid them. You'll learn how to advocate for yourself, grow your skills, prepare for unexpected changes, and protect your professional reputation. A thoughtful approach to your career can help you build both financial confidence and long-term security.

NOT NEGOTIATING SALARIES

The Situation:

Megan landed her dream job right out of college. Excited to start, she accepted the first salary offer without question. A year later, she discovered that her coworkers with similar experience were earning 10% more because they had negotiated their offers. Megan felt undervalued and struggled to catch up financially, even after receiving small raises.

The Mistake:

Accepting the first salary offer without negotiation can leave you earning less than your true value, affecting long-term savings, retirement contributions, and overall financial stability.

The Solutions:

- **Do Your Research** - Use resources like Glassdoor, Payscale, or LinkedIn Salary Insights to understand industry standards for your position.

- **Practice Your Pitch** - Prepare to highlight your skills, achievements, and the value you bring to the company. Use the Salary/Raise Request Prep List in this Chapter's Appendix.

- **Negotiate Benefits** - If the salary is fixed, consider negotiating perks like remote work options, bonuses, extra vacation days, or professional development budgets.

- **Be Confident but Flexible** - Approach negotiations professionally and remain open to compromise if needed.

FAILING TO PLAN FOR JOB LOSS

The Situation:

When Ryan was unexpectedly laid off, he had no savings and no other sources of income. With bills piling up, he quickly burned through his credit cards and fell into debt. It took him months to find a new job, and by then, his credit score had taken a hit, and his confidence was shaken.

The Mistake:

Not having an emergency fund or backup income leaves you vulnerable during unexpected job losses, leading to debt and financial instability.

The Solutions:

- **Build an Emergency Fund** - Save 3–6 months' worth of expenses to cover job loss or emergencies. See the Emergency Fund Builder in the Appendix for Chapter 5.

- **Create Multiple Income Streams** - Develop side gigs, freelance work, or passive income sources to reduce reliance on a single paycheck.

- **Keep Your Resume Updated** - Regularly refresh your resume and LinkedIn profile to stay prepared for job hunting.

- **Network Consistently and Constantly** - Build relationships within your industry to increase job opportunities if needed.

QUITTING WITHOUT NOTICE

The Situation:

After a heated argument with her manager, Sienna quit her job on the spot. While the decision provided short-term relief, it hurt her professionally. She struggled to get positive references and explain her abrupt departure in interviews.

The Mistake:

Quitting without proper notice can damage your reputation, burn bridges, and make it harder to secure future job opportunities.

The Solutions:

- **Think Before Acting** - Take time to evaluate the situation and consider alternatives like transferring departments or discussing issues with HR.

- **Give Proper Notice** - Provide at least two weeks' notice and help with transitioning your workload to leave on good terms. See the Two-Week Notice Template in this Chapter's Appendix.

- **Secure References Before Leaving** - Ask for recommendations and build a positive exit narrative to share during future interviews.

- **Plan Your Transition** - Ensure you have another job lined up or enough savings before making a decision to leave.

AVOIDING CAREER DEVELOPMENT

The Situation:

Owen stayed in the same job for over eight years without pursuing additional training or certifications. When a promotion opportunity came up, he was passed over for a coworker who had taken professional development courses and attended industry conferences. Owen realized too late that his lack of growth had held him back.

The Mistake:

Failing to invest in skills and education can make you less competitive in the job market and limit career advancement opportunities both with your current employer and if you seek employment elsewhere in the future.

The Solutions:

- **Commit to Lifelong Learning** - Take online courses, attend workshops, or earn certifications to stay updated in your field.

- **Seek Feedback** - Regularly ask supervisors for input on areas for improvement and growth. Accept their comments as constructive criticism, make appropriate changes and don't take anything they say personally.

- **Set Career Goals** - Develop a long-term career plan and identify the skills you need to achieve it.

- **Leverage Employer Resources** - Use company-sponsored programs for education or professional development whenever available.

STAYING IN A DEAD-END JOB TOO LONG

The Situation:

Lena had been with the same company for over twelve years. While she appreciated the stability, her role hadn't changed in years, her salary had barely increased, and there were no opportunities for advancement. She often thought about looking for something new but felt loyal to her coworkers and feared the uncertainty of starting over. Years later, she realized she had missed out on higher income, better benefits, and more fulfilling work.

The Mistake:

Staying in a job with no growth potential due to fear, complacency, or misplaced loyalty can limit your income, skills, and career satisfaction. It may also prevent you from building a stronger financial future.

The Solutions:

- **Evaluate Regularly** - Assess your role and growth opportunities at least once a year.

- **Know Your Worth** - Research salaries in your industry to see if you are being compensated fairly.

- **Invest in Growth** - Take courses, attend workshops, or earn certifications to keep your skills current.

- **Create an Exit Strategy** - Set a timeline and plan for finding new opportunities. Set short-term and long- term goals for yourself. Look into any additional education or certifications you could obtain.

- **Don't Let Fear Decide** - Change can be uncomfortable, but staying stuck has long-term costs.

NOT UNDERSTANDING YOUR BENEFITS PACKAGE

The Situation:

Jackson landed a great new job with a solid salary and quickly focused on getting up to speed with work responsibilities. But he never took the time to read through his employee benefits package. A year later, he discovered he had missed out on thousands in unclaimed 401(k) matching contributions and didn't realize his health plan came with an HSA option that could have saved him money on medical expenses and could have reduced his taxable income.

The Mistake:

Overlooking or underutilizing your employee benefits means leaving free money and valuable tax advantages on the table. Not understanding your options can also lead to choosing the wrong health coverage or missing deadlines for savings opportunities.

The Solutions:

- **Review Your Benefits Annually** - Take time during open enrollment to understand what's offered and how to maximize it.

- **Max Out Employer Matches** - Contribute enough to your 401(k) to receive the full employer match - it's free money.

- **Use Pre-Tax Savings Tools** - Take advantage of HSAs and FSAs to reduce taxable income and plan for healthcare costs.

- **Ask HR for Clarification** - Don't guess and don't be embarrassed to get help understanding what's available and how it works.

- **Revisit as Life Changes** - Reevaluate your benefits when you get married, have a child, or experience a major life event.

BURNING BRIDGES

The Situation:

After months of frustration with his manager, Charlie decided to quit his job without giving notice. He sent a brief resignation email and never looked back. He also bashed his employer online and to others in the industry. At the time, it felt empowering but months later, he regretted it. A potential employer asked for a reference from his previous job, and he realized he had damaged a relationship that could have helped his career long-term.

The Mistake:

Leaving a job on bad terms or without notice can damage your professional reputation, limit your network, and hurt future job prospects, especially in tight-knit industries.

The Solutions:

- **Give Proper Notice** - Aim for two weeks' notice (or more) whenever possible to maintain professionalism. See the Two-Week Notice Template in this Chapter's Appendix.

- **Exit Gracefully -** Leave a positive final impression by tying up loose ends and offering a smooth transition.

- **Keep Emotions in Check -** Even if you're upset, avoid burning bridges through angry emails or dramatic exits. That may work in the movies but not in real life!

- **Stay Connected -** Thank coworkers and supervisors before you go, and consider staying connected on social media sites.

- **Think Long-Term -** Treat every job as a stepping stone; you never know when you will cross paths again.

MISMANAGING A SIDE HUSTLE

The Situation:

Valerie started selling homemade candles on weekends to earn extra income. At first, sales were steady, and she felt confident it would be a great financial boost. But by year's end, she realized she hadn't kept receipts, didn't track income properly, and hadn't set aside any money for taxes. She also used her personal checking account for all business transactions, which made filing taxes and figuring out if she even made a profit a complete mess.

The Mistake:

Overestimating profits, underestimating taxes, and failing to separate personal and business finances can turn a promising side hustle into a financial headache. Many new entrepreneurs forget that side income is still taxable and must be tracked like a real business.

The Solutions:

- **Open a Separate Business Bank Account** - Keep all income and expenses separate from your personal finances to stay organized.

- **Track Everything** - Use simple accounting tools or spreadsheets to track income, costs, and mileage. Save receipts for all business purchases.

- **Plan for Taxes** - Set aside 25-30% of your side hustle income for self-employment taxes and consider making quarterly estimated payments.

- **Know What Counts as Income** - Even payments through Venmo, PayPal, or cash apps must be reported to the IRS.

- **Don't Assume You're Profitable** - Calculate your actual net income after expenses, taxes, and time. A high sales total doesn't mean you're making money.

CHAPTER 8:
SCAMS AND FRAUD

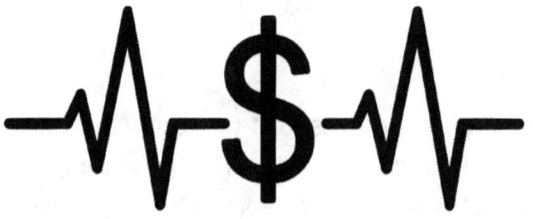

Scams and fraud are nothing new. In fact, they've been around for centuries. However, in today's digital world, they're more sophisticated, more convincing, and more widespread than ever. With a few clicks, scammers can send deceptive messages, pose as trusted contacts, or create fake investment opportunities that look completely legitimate. These schemes prey on emotions like urgency, fear, and greed. They can catch even the most cautious person off guard. A single misstep can result in stolen money, damaged credit, and even identity theft.

The rise of artificial intelligence has made things even trickier. Deepfake calls, AI-generated messages, and ultra-realistic phishing attempts make it harder to tell what's real. Whether it's an urgent email about a "suspicious account login," a fake social media giveaway, or a convincing pitch for an investment that promises quick returns, these scams are designed to exploit your trust and your wallet.

In this chapter, we'll walk through the most common (and newest) types of scams, share real-life stories, and show you how simple steps can protect you and your loved ones. You'll learn how to spot red flags, safeguard your personal information, and make decisions rooted in logic and not pressure. Our goal here is not to increase your paranoia but to stress that with a little bit of preparation, you can stay vigilant and help your friends and family stay vigilant as well. Awareness is your best defense!

FALLING FOR ONLINE SCAMS

The Situation:

Parker received an email claiming he had won a $5,000 prize. All he had to do was pay a small 10% "processing fee" to claim it. Excited, he wired the money and waited for his prize to arrive. It never did. He later realized he had been scammed and lost $500.

The Mistake:

Sending money or personal information to unverified offers can result in financial loss and identity theft.

The Solutions:

- **Verify Sources** - Never trust unsolicited emails, messages, or calls. Research companies and offers before responding.

- **Look for Red Flags** - Be wary of high-pressure tactics, spelling errors, and requests for payment via gift cards or wire transfers.

- **Use Security Software** - Install antivirus and anti-phishing tools to protect your devices.

- **Report Scams** - Notify the Federal Trade Commission (FTC) and your bank if you suspect fraud. See the Fraud Alert Checklist in this Chapter's Appendix.

FALLING FOR SOPHISTICATED AND AI-DRIVEN SCAMS

The Situation:

Rita received a frantic phone call from someone who sounded exactly like her grandson. He claimed to be in trouble, needed money urgently, and begged her not to tell anyone. Fearing for his safety, she wired $5,000 immediately. Later, she discovered her grandson was perfectly fine and that scammers had used artificial intelligence to clone his voice. The emotional stress and financial loss were devastating.

The Mistake:

As scams become more sophisticated with AI-generated voices, deepfake videos, and convincing phishing emails, many people fall victim by reacting emotionally instead of verifying the source. Believing what sounds or looks real without confirming it can lead to major financial as well as identity theft losses.

The Solutions:

- **Pause and Verify** - If someone claims to be a loved one in trouble, hang up and call them or a trusted contact directly before sending money.

- **Create a Family Code Word -** Share a secret phrase with loved ones that can be used to confirm identity in emergencies. Ask a personal question that only that person can answer correctly to ensure that's who you're talking to.

- **Be Cautious with Personal Info Online -** Scammers scrape social media for names, voices, and habits to personalize attacks. Do a

Social Media Audit and look at who your friends and connections are. Don't be afraid or embarrassed to delete people you don't know or recognize. Use the Privacy Settings most social media sites offer to limit who has access to your posts and information.

- **Enable Call Screening and Email Filters -** Use spam blockers, antivirus protection, and caller ID to reduce exposure.

- **Stay Informed and Educated -** Learn about emerging scams and educate family members, especially older adults, who may be more vulnerable. Use the Fraud Filter Checklist in this Chapter's Appendix to learn how to spot a scam before it's too late.

INVESTING IN GET-RICH-QUICK SCHEMES

The Situation:

Dominic was introduced to an investment opportunity from an acquaintance promising a 50% return in just a few months. Skeptical at first, he eventually gave in after hearing testimonials from other investors. After investing $10,000, he discovered it was a Ponzi scheme and lost everything.

The Mistake:

Trusting unrealistic promises of high returns often leads to financial losses and heartbreak.

The Solutions:

- **Investigate Before Investing -** Research investment opportunities thoroughly, including checking licenses and reviews. Use the Investment Red Flag Worksheet in this Chapter's Appendix to evaluate an investment offer or opportunity.

- **Follow the Rule of Thumb** - If it sounds too good to be true, it probably is.

- **Consult a Professional** - Work with licensed financial advisors or seek legal advice to vet investment opportunities.

- **Diversify Investments** - Spread your investments across multiple assets to reduce risk.

SHARING PERSONAL INFORMATION CARELESSLY

The Situation:

Tom received a call from someone claiming to be from his bank, asking for his Social Security number to verify suspicious activity. Panicked, he provided the information, only to discover later that his identity had been stolen and fraudulent charges appeared on his accounts.

The Mistake:

Sharing sensitive information without verifying the source exposes you to identity theft and financial fraud.

The Solutions:

- **Verify Callers** - Never share personal information over the phone or email without confirming the source. Call the organization directly using official contact information.

- **Use Strong Passwords -** Create unique passwords for each account and enable two-factor authentication. See the Everyday Practices That Make Cyber Sense in this Chapter's Appendix for staying safe online with simple, smart habits anyone can follow.

- **Monitor Accounts -** Regularly review bank and credit card statements for suspicious activity.

- **Freeze Your Credit -** Prevent unauthorized access to your credit by placing a freeze with major credit bureaus.

BUYING UNVERIFIED CRYPTOCURRENCY

The Situation:

Claire kept seeing posts on social media about a trending cryptocurrency that was "guaranteed to explode" in value. Influencers were hyping it, and even some of her friends were jumping in, so she did too. Without fully understanding how it worked or who was behind it, she invested $2,000. Within weeks, the value crashed, and the project vanished. It turned out to be a pump-and-dump scheme, and Claire was left with nothing.

The Mistake:

Investing in speculative or unverified cryptocurrency without understanding the risks can lead to significant losses.

The Solutions:

- **Research Thoroughly** - Only invest in established cryptocurrencies with clear documentation and credible teams.

- **Avoid Hype-Driven Decisions -** Don't make investment decisions based on social media trends or celebrity endorsements.

- **Use Reputable Platforms -** Stick to well-known exchanges and wallets with strong security measures.

- **Invest What You Can Afford to Lose -** Cryptocurrency is highly volatile and unpredictable. Prices can swing wildly in a short period, and some coins may lose all their value. Because of this risk, it's wise to invest only a small portion of your money, an amount you could afford to lose, without it affecting your financial stability or long-term goals. Think of it more like a gamble than a guaranteed investment.

CHAPTER 9:

RELATIONSHIP AND EMOTIONAL MONEY MISTAKES

Money and emotions are closely connected, especially when it comes to the people we care about. Whether it's lending money to a friend, paying for a loved one's debt, or combining finances too soon, our feelings can sometimes cloud our judgment. Decisions made out of love, guilt, obligation, or trust can end up creating long-term stress, debt, and even fractured relationships if we're not careful.

In relationships, money mistakes often stem from the desire to help or avoid conflict. But without clear communication and boundaries, these well-meaning actions can lead to resentment and financial instability. Emotional spending, relying on verbal promises, or supporting loved ones at your own expense are all signs that feelings are overriding smart financial decisions. Being generous or trusting isn't a flaw but protecting your financial health is just as important as protecting your relationships.

In this chapter, we'll explore common emotional and relationship-based money mistakes and offer practical ways to avoid them. You'll learn how to spot warning signs, set healthy boundaries, and create agreements that keep everyone on the same page. With a little planning and honest conversation, you can protect both your finances and the connections that matter most.

COMBINING FINANCES WITHOUT PLANNING

The Situation:

When Lorenzo and Leah got married, they combined their bank accounts without discussing spending habits or financial goals. Leah was a saver, but Lorenzo enjoyed indulging in expensive hobbies and always had to have the latest gadgets, no matter the cost. Arguments about money soon became frequent, leading to resentment and stress.

The Mistake:

Merging finances without clear agreements can create misunderstandings and strain relationships.

The Solutions:

- **Discuss Money Early and Often -** Have open conversations about spending habits, debts, and goals before combining finances whether it's with your life partner, spouse or even a new roommate. Some people say it's an awkward and difficult discussion to have but honestly, it can only help in the long run. Use the Money Talk Conversation Guide in this Chapter's Appendix to help you steer the conversation.

- **Create a Joint Budget -** Develop a shared plan for expenses, savings, and investments. Use the Joint Expense Agreement in this Chapter's Appendix.

- **Maintain Some Independence -** Keep individual accounts for personal spending while using a joint account for shared expenses.

- **Set Boundaries and Financial Ground Rules -** Establish spending limits and require mutual approval for large purchases.

PAYING FOR OTHERS' FINANCIAL MISTAKES

The Situation:

Jonah's brother frequently borrowed money to cover rent and bills, promising to pay it back. Jonah felt obligated to help, but the repayments never came. After years of bailing him out, Jonah was deep in debt and his brother still hadn't changed his spending habits.

The Mistake:

Covering someone else's financial mistakes often enables bad behavior and puts your own finances at risk.

The Solutions:

- **Set Boundaries** - Offer non-monetary help, like budgeting advice or job referrals, instead of cash.

- **Establish Clear Terms** - If you do lend money, create a written agreement with repayment terms.

- **Say No Without Guilt** - Prioritize your financial health and recognize that enabling a loved one's bad habits doesn't solve the problem.

- **Encourage Accountability** - Suggest professional financial counseling or debt management programs.

LETTING EMOTIONS DRIVE SPENDING

The Situation:

After a tough breakup, Josephine turned to shopping to lift her spirits. Over the next few months, she spent thousands on clothes, gadgets, and vacations she couldn't afford. When the credit card bills arrived, her emotional spending spree left her feeling even worse.

The Mistake:

Emotional spending often leads to regret, debt, and guilt, creating a cycle that's hard to break.

The Solutions:

- **Pause Before Buying** - Implement a 24-hour rule to avoid impulsive purchases.

- **Find Healthy Outlets** - Replace shopping with activities like exercise, journaling, or spending time with loved ones.

- **Create a Fun Money Budget** - Set aside a specific amount each month for guilt-free spending to prevent splurges.

- **Track Spending Patterns** - Use budgeting apps to monitor and control emotional spending habits.

TRUSTING TOO MUCH IN VERBAL PROMISES

The Situation:

Grace lent $3,000 to a coworker who promised to pay it back within three months. The repayment never happened, and the coworker left the company without a trace. Grace had no written agreement and no way to recover her money.

The Mistake:

Relying on verbal agreements instead of formal contracts can lead to disputes and financial losses.

The Solutions:

- **Always Get It in Writing** - Create a simple promissory note outlining repayment terms, interest (if any), and due dates. Make sure you also have the person's address, phone number and email address.

- **Use Payment Platforms** - Send money through apps that track transactions rather than cash.

- **Consult a Lawyer for Large Loans** - For significant amounts, draft legal agreements to protect yourself.

- **Be Prepared to Walk Away** - If terms can't be agreed upon, consider saying no to the request.

FINANCIAL ENABLING LOVED ONES

The Situation:

Lily and her husband were nearing retirement when their adult son, Ben, lost his job. Wanting to help, they began covering his rent, car payment, and even his credit card bills "just until he got back on his feet." Months turned into years, and while Ben made minimal effort to find stable work, Lily and her husband delayed their retirement plans and tapped into their savings. They didn't realize they had slipped into the role of "snow plow parents" - clearing every obstacle out of their son's path at the cost of their own financial future.

The Mistake:

Financial enabling, continuously rescuing adult children or family members from the consequences of their money decisions, can create long-term dependency. It often delays their financial maturity while jeopardizing your own savings, retirement, and peace of mind.

The Solutions:

- **Set Boundaries with Love -** Support doesn't have to mean financial handouts. Offer emotional encouragement and practical advice instead of cash.

- **Give a Clear Timeline -** If financial help is necessary, set firm expectations: how much you'll give, for how long, and what the recipient is expected to do in return.

- **Avoid Guilt-Based Giving -** Helping others shouldn't leave you financially insecure. Remember: your stability matters too. It's one thing to pay for a family vacation for your children and grandchildren if you are financially able to do so, and a whole other ball game to provide ongoing financial support for their bills, housing, or debt.

- **Encourage Financial Growth -** Instead of bailing them out, help them build a budget, find work, or seek credit counseling.

- **Have the Hard Conversations -** Let loved ones know you're stepping back to protect your own future, and stick to the plan, no matter how uncomfortable of a conversation it is. Use the Family Boundaries and Budget Agreement Template in this Chapter's Appendix to outline expectations and encourage accountability.

CONCLUSION

YOUR FINANCIAL FUTURE STARTS NOW

Congratulations! You've taken a significant step toward mastering your finances and avoiding costly mistakes. Whether you've identified areas to improve or discovered strategies to reinforce your existing habits, you're now equipped with the tools and insights to make smarter financial decisions.

Throughout this book, we've explored the most common money mistakes - from borrowing, spending and investing pitfalls to career missteps, tax blunders, and emotional financial decisions. These lessons were not just about avoiding errors but about teaching you to take charge of your financial life with confidence.

THE POWER OF PROGRESS

Remember, success isn't about perfection - it's about progress. Mistakes happen, but what matters most is learning from them and making adjustments. Every step you take, no matter how small, moves you closer to financial security and independence.

You've already proven your commitment to improving your financial literacy by reading this book. Now it's time to take what you've learned and put it into action.

PRACTICAL STEPS MOVING FORWARD

- Review and Reflect - Go back through the chapters and revisit the areas where you felt most vulnerable. Highlight key strategies you want to prioritize.

- Set Financial Goals - Define short-term and long-term goals, whether it's building an emergency fund, paying off debt, or saving for retirement. Use the worksheets and tools in the Appendix to create actionable plans.

- Monitor Your Progress - Regularly track spending, review your credit score, and adjust your budget to stay aligned with your goals.

- Keep Learning - Financial literacy is an ongoing journey. Stay informed by reading books, listening to podcasts, and attending workshops. Knowledge is your best defense against costly mistakes.

- Share What You've Learned - Help friends and family avoid financial pitfalls by sharing the lessons from this book. Encourage them to build better habits and start their own financial journeys.

A FINAL WORD OF ENCOURAGEMENT

You don't have to be a financial expert to build a secure future. All it takes is the right knowledge and mindset, using the appropriate tools and having the willingness to take action. Mistakes may be part of the journey, but they don't have to define it. Each chapter of this book was designed to help you identify and fix the most common money missteps when they happen and teach you to avoid them in the future.

Your financial story is still being written, and you have the power to shape it. Start by applying the lessons in this book, stay focused on your goals, and celebrate every milestone along the way.

Thank you for trusting this book as your guide. Financial freedom starts with knowledge and now you have it. Keep going, stay curious, and pass this book along to someone who could use a little more Dollars and Sense in their life.

CHAPTER 1 APPENDIX:
MONEY MINDSET FINANCIAL FIRST AID KIT

LIMITING BELIEFS TO EMPOWERING REFRAME CHART

Our beliefs shape our decisions, and nowhere is that truer than with money. Many of us carry hidden, negative beliefs we have picked up from childhood, society, or past financial struggles. We believe that we're "just not good with money" or that we'll "always be broke." These beliefs create mental roadblocks that lead to procrastination, fear, and most damaging of all - financial self-sabotage.

Reframing is the practice of taking those limiting beliefs and replacing them with more accurate, empowering thoughts that support growth and progress. This chart helps readers recognize their inner dialogue and rewire it to support healthier financial behavior.

Read each limiting belief slowly and ask yourself: Have I ever thought or felt this way? If so, repeat the empowering reframe. And repeat that reframe every time you catch the old limiting belief thought creeping back in!

Limiting Belief	Empowering Reframe
I'm bad with money.	I'm learning to manage my money better every day.
I'll never get out of debt.	I'm taking small steps toward becoming debt-free.
I don't make enough to save.	I can start small and build savings over time.
I'm too old to learn this.	It's never too late to take control of my finances.
I always mess up with money.	I've made mistakes, but I'm going to learn and improve.
I'll never be wealthy.	I can build wealth in my own time and in my own way.
Money matters stress me out.	I'm learning how to make money matters feel manageable.
People like me don't succeed financially.	Financial success is possible for me since I am willing to learn.

CHAPTER 2 APPENDIX:

BORROWING AND LENDING FINANCIAL FIRST AID KIT

PROMISSORY NOTE TEMPLATE

Borrower Information:	Name: _____
	Address: _____
	Phone: _____
	Email address: _____
Lender Information:	Name: _____
	Address: _____
	Phone: _____
	Email address: _____

| Loan Terms: Loan Amount: $_____ | Interest Rate (Annual): _____ % |

[If no interest is charged, write "This is a zero-interest loan"]

Repayment Schedule: (Ex: $ 100 per month by Zelle on the 5th day of each month, starting mm/dd/yy)
_____

| Late Payment Penalty (if any): $_____ | if payment is more than _____ days late. |

Prepayment Clause:

☐   Borrower may prepay the loan without penalty.

☐   Borrower may not prepay without prior consent from the lender.

Default Clause: Failure to pay as agreed will result in the full loan amount becoming immediately due and lender may take legal action.

This Note shall be governed and construed under the laws of the State of _____

Signatures

| _____ | _____ |
| Borrower Signature & Date | Lender Signature & Date |

_____
Witness/Notary Signature (Optional)

CHAPTER 3 APPENDIX:

SPENDING FINANCIAL FIRST AID KIT

IMPULSE SPENDING TRACKER (30 DAY LOG)

Fill in each row after every unplanned purchase. At the end of the 30 days, review for patterns to identify common emotional or situational triggers.

DATE	ITEM PURCHASED	COST	WAS IT A WANT OR A NEED?	WHAT TRIGGERED THE PURCHASE? [*email, TV ad, website, stress, hunger, boredom*]	HOW DID YOU FEEL AFTER?	WOULD YOU BUY THIS ITEM AGAIN?

SMART SHOPPING LIST TEMPLATE

(Use this before heading to the store or shopping online)

Needs/Must Haves/Essentials

(Things you actually need based on your meal planning, household needs or personal care)

Wants/Nice-to-Haves

(Think twice before buying! Add to shopping cart only after your NEEDS are covered)

MONTHLY BUDGET TEMPLATE
(NEEDS/WANTS/SAVE AND DEBT REPAYMENT)

This monthly budget template helps you take control of your finances by dividing your spending into three key categories: Needs, Wants, and Savings/Debt Repayment. The "Needs" section covers essentials like housing, groceries, and transportation - things you must pay for to live and work. The "Wants" section includes non-essentials like dining out, entertainment, and shopping - fun extras that make life enjoyable. The final section is for building financial security through saving and paying down debt. By tracking income and expenses this way, you can make smarter choices and stay on top of your money.

The 50/30/20 rule is a simple budgeting guideline that helps you manage your money by dividing your after-tax income into three main categories: 50% for Needs, 30% for Wants and 20% for Savings and Debt Repayment.

By following the 50/30/20 rule, you create a balanced spending plan that covers your essentials, allows room for enjoyment, and keeps your financial future on track.

First, identify your income and divide the total monthly amount into 50%, 30% and 20%.

INCOME

Source	Amount
Primary Job	$
Other	$
Other	$
Other	$
Other	$
Total Monthly Income	$
50% of Monthly Income - Allocated for Needs	$
30% of Monthly Income - Allocated for Wants	$
20% of Monthly Income - Allocated for Savings/Debt	$

Next, identify your essential expenses - your needs

EXPENSES - NEEDS (Essentials: Should be 50% of Income or Less)

Category	Amount	Notes
Housing (Rent/Mortgage)	$	
Utilities (Electric/Gas/Water)	$	
Groceries	$	
Transportation (Gas/Bus/Train)	$	
Insurance (Health/Auto)	$	
Loan Payments (Auto/Credit Card Minimums)	$	
Childcare/School Tuition	$	
Phone/Internet	$	
Other	$	
Other	$	
Total Monthly Needs	$	

Now, identify your lifestyle expenses - your wants

EXPENSES - WANTS (Lifestyle: Should be 30% of Income or Less)

Category	Amount	Notes
Dining Out	$	
Subscriptions	$	
Shopping	$	
Entertainment	$	
Travel/Vacation	$	
Hobbies/Leisure Activities	$	
Other	$	
Other	$	
Total Monthly Wants	$	

Finally, list your extra debt payments to reduce your debt balances (think credit card balances) and your savings as well as retirement goals

EXPENSES – SAVINGS & DEBT REPAYMENT (Should be AT LEAST 20% of Income)

Category	Amount	Notes
Extra Debt Payments (Towards balances)	$	
Emergency Fund	$	
Retirement Savings	$	
Investments	$	
Specific Goal Saving Fund (Vacation)	$	
Specific Goal Saving Fund (Major Purchase)	$	
Other	$	
Other	$	
Total Monthly Savings & Debt Repayment	$	

The purpose of breaking down your income and expenses is to show you a clear picture of where your money is going. Once you've tallied the above, use that information to create a realistic budget.

Creating a budget is important to make sure you're putting money towards what matters most. The goal is to ensure your spending aligns with your priorities, helps you avoid overspending, and allows you to plan ahead for emergencies and future goals.

No budget is set in stone. Life is unpredictable, and your financial needs and goals may shift from month to month. A good budget should be flexible, allowing you to make adjustments as circumstances change whether it's an unexpected expense, a change in income, or new financial priorities. For example, if your car breaks down and you need a costly repair, you might need to temporarily reduce spending on dining out or entertainment to cover it.

Regularly reviewing and updating your budget ensures it stays realistic and relevant, helping you stay in control of your money without feeling restricted.

Think of your budget as a living plan that evolves with you.

HOMEOWNER COST BREAKDOWN WORKSHEET

Use this worksheet to estimate and track the real monthly and annual costs of owning a home beyond just the mortgage. Use it before purchasing a home to assess its affordability and revisit it annually for planning.

Expense Category	Estimated Monthly Cost	Estimated Annual Cost	Notes
Mortgage Payment (Principal + Interest)			Based on loan terms
Property Taxes			May be included in escrow
Homeowners Insurance			Compare quotes annually
Private Mortgage Insurance (PMI)			If down payment is less than 20%
Utilities (Gas, Electric, Water)			May vary seasonally
Trash & Sewer Fees			Sometimes separate from water bill
HOA Fees (if applicable)			Check for annual increases
Maintenance & Repairs			Budget 1-3% of home value per year
Landscaping or Lawn Care			Equipment, service, or seasonal cleanup
Pest Control			Optional but wise in some areas
Appliance Replacement Fund			Average lifespan of an appliance is 8-15 years
Roof, HVAC, and Plumbing Reserve			Have a reserve savings fund specifically for these expensive repairs.
Home Improvements/ Upgrades			Discretionary but common
Security System Monitoring			Optional but increasingly common
Emergency Fund for Unexpected Issues			For floods, leaks, break-ins, etc.

QUARTERLY SUBSCRIPTION AUDIT

A subscription audit is a smart habit to build into your routine every quarter. Over time, it's easy to accumulate multiple streaming services, apps, memberships, and recurring charges that quietly drain your bank account. Set aside time every three months to review your bank and credit card statements for any automatic payments. Ask yourself: Do I still use this? Is it worth the cost? Could I pause or cancel it? Even small monthly fees can add up significantly over a year. Canceling unused or unnecessary subscriptions is a simple way to cut waste and redirect that money toward savings or more meaningful expenses. Conduct this audit quarterly and slowly eliminate waste!

Service Name	Monthly Cost	Last Used	Priority (High/Medium/Low)	Cancel or Keep	Notes

CASH RECEIPT TEMPLATE

Date of Payment: _____
Amount Paid: $_____
Received By (Recipient Name): _____
Received For (Payor Name): _____
Purpose of Payment: _____
Additional Notes: _____   _____   _____
Signatures

_____	_____
Recipient Signature & Date	Payor Signature & Date

CHAPTER 4 APPENDIX:

DEBT AND CREDIT FINANCIAL FIRST AID KIT

MINIMUM PAYMENT INTEREST CALCULATOR

Making only the minimum payment on your credit card each month might seem manageable but it can cost you thousands in interest and take years to pay off. Follow these step-by-step instructions to see the real cost of carrying a balance. This tool has the potential to be the biggest wake-up call to help you take control of your debt.

Step 1: Gather Your Credit Card Statements

You'll need the following details for each one:

- Total Balance Owed

- Interest Rate (APR) - usually listed as a percentage

- Minimum Monthly Payment - either a fixed amount or a percentage of the balance

Step 2: Run the Calculation

Use any online calculator to estimate:

- How long it will take to pay off the card if you only pay the minimum

- How much total interest you'll pay over that time

- How much faster you can pay it off with just $25-$100 extra per month

DEBT PAYOFF TRACKER

This Debt Payoff Tracker is designed to help you take control by listing each of your debts, organizing key details like balances, interest rates, and due dates, and choosing a repayment strategy that works best for your situation. Whether you use the **Snowball Method** *(paying off the smallest balances first to build momentum) or the* **Avalanche Method** *(tackling the highest interest rates to save money over time), this tool gives you a structured way to track your efforts. By updating this chart monthly, you'll stay motivated, watch your debt going down, and get one step closer to a debt-free future.*

Creditor	Account Type (Credit Card/ Loan)	Balance	Interest Rate	Strategy to use (Snowball/ Avalanche)	Notes

CREDIT REPORT REVIEW CHECKLIST

Your credit report is a snapshot of your financial reputation and it's important to make sure it's accurate. Use this checklist to request your reports, review key sections (like payment history and credit inquiries), and take action to dispute errors or outdated items. To monitor your credit year-round, stagger your free credit report requests by ordering one from each of the three major bureaus (Equifax, Experian, TransUnion) every four months. This way, you can keep an eye on changes or errors without waiting an entire year. Keeping your credit clean is essential for better interest rates, housing, and job opportunities.

Get Your Credit Reports for FREE using ONLY the website AnnualCreditReport.com

☐	Equifax	Date Ordered _____
☐	Experian	Date Ordered _____
☐	TransUnion	Date Ordered _____

Review These Sections on Each Report

Section	Review Complete	Issues Found	Notes or Dispute Status
Personal Information	□ Yes	□ Yes	
Open Accounts	□ Yes	□ Yes	
Closed Accounts	□ Yes	□ Yes	
Late Payments	□ Yes	□ Yes	
Collections	□ Yes	□ Yes	
Hard Inquiries	□ Yes	□ Yes	
Public Records	□ Yes	□ Yes	

If you find errors, submit disputes online with each bureau, follow up regularly and note your dispute status here.

DUE DATE CALENDAR TEMPLATE

Missing payment deadlines can hurt your credit score and rack up late fees. Use this monthly calendar template to list all of your due dates - credit cards, loans, utilities, and other bills - and to make sure you have set up Auto-Pay to avoid missing any payments. Place it somewhere visible or sync it with your phone to stay on top of your obligations and maintain financial peace of mind.

Bill/Account	Due Date	Auto-Pay set up	Notes
		☐ Yes	
		☐ Yes	
		☐ Yes	
		☐ Yes	
		☐ Yes	
		☐ Yes	
		☐ Yes	

CHAPTER 5 APPENDIX:
SAVINGS AND INVESTING FINANCIAL FIRST AID KIT

EMERGENCY FUND BUILDER

Step 1: List Fixed Monthly Expenses

Expense Type	Monthly Amount
Rent/Mortgage	$
Utilities	$
Groceries	$
Insurance (Health, Auto, etc.)	$
Transportation	$
Loan Payments	$
Other Essentials	$
Total Monthly Expenses	**$**

Step 2: Choose Savings Goal – Multiply Total Monthly Expenses by 3 and by 6

Goal Length	Target Amount
3 Months	$
6 Months	$

Step 3: Determine Monthly Savings Amount

3 Months Target Amount	Months to Save	Monthly Goal
$		$
6 Months Target Amount	**Months to Save**	**Monthly Goal**
$		$

CHAPTER 6 APPENDIX:

TAX AND LEGAL FINANCIAL FIRST AID KIT

TAX DOCUMENT CHECKLIST

Personal Information

- ☐ Social Security Numbers (self, spouse, dependents)
- ☐ ID (Driver's License, Birth Certificates)
- ☐ Prior Year's Tax Return

Income Documents

- ☐ W-2s (Wages, Salary)
- ☐ 1099-NEC or 1099-MISC (Freelance/Contract Work)
- ☐ 1099-INT, 1099-DIV (Interest, Dividends)
- ☐ 1099-G (Unemployment or State Refunds)
- ☐ 1099-R (Retirement distributions)
- ☐ 1099-B or 1099-K (Investments or online sales)
- ☐ K-1s (Partnerships, Trusts)
- ☐ W2-G (Certain Gambling Winnings)

Adjustments & Deductions

- ☐ Student loan interest
- ☐ IRA contributions
- ☐ Educator expenses
- ☐ HSA contributions

Credits and Itemized Deductions

- ☐ Childcare expenses (with provider info)

- ☐ Charitable contributions (with receipts)
- ☐ Medical and dental expenses
- ☐ Mortgage interest (Form 1098)
- ☐ Property tax bills
- ☐ Education expenses (Form 1098-T)
- ☐ Home office deduction info

Other

- ☐ Amount and Dates of Estimated tax payments
- ☐ Bank account info for direct deposit
- ☐ Any IRS or state letters received

CHARITABLE CONTRIBUTIONS LOG

Date	Organization Name	Type of Donation (Cash, Check, Credit Card, Goods, Services)	Amount/Items Donated	Notes

Keep this log updated monthly so you're not scrambling at tax time.

You can also customize this log for any major or work-related expenses that you think may be deductible.

BASIC WILL & ESTATE ORGANIZER

This worksheet is designed to help you gather and organize essential information about your assets, beneficiaries, and final wishes. It serves as a practical starting point meant to clarify your intentions and make future planning easier for both you and your loved ones. Please note that this organizer is not a substitute for a valid will or legal estate plan. Laws regarding wills, probate, and estate distribution vary by state, and only a licensed attorney in your jurisdiction can provide the proper legal guidance to ensure your wishes are carried out legally and effectively. Use this worksheet to prepare for that important conversation.

1. Personal Information

Name: _____

Date of Birth: _____

Address: _____

2. Executor of Will

Name: _____

Contact Info: _____

3. Beneficiaries (Names, Dates of Birth, Relationship, Asset(s) Assigned)

4. Assets to Include

☐   Bank Accounts

☐   Real Estate

☐   Retirement Accounts

- ☐   Life Insurance Policies
- ☐   Vehicles
- ☐   Jewelry, Art, Collectibles, Family Heirlooms

5. Digital Assets

- ☐   Email accounts
- ☐   Social media profiles
- ☐   Online banking logins
- ☐   Digital files (photos, documents)

6. Other Instructions

Funeral Preferences

Guardians for Children

POWER OF ATTORNEY AUTHORIZATION TEMPLATE

*This Power of Attorney (POA) Authorization Template is a simple, fill-in-the-blank tool to help you begin thinking about who should legally act on your behalf in the event you're unable to make decisions yourself and what decisions you are giving them the ability to make. It is **not** a legally binding document but rather an organizational worksheet designed to help you clarify your preferences before meeting with a qualified attorney. A POA can give someone the authority to make financial, medical, legal, or other decisions for you, making it one of the most important legal tools in long-term planning. Because each state has different laws regarding how POAs must be executed and when they take effect, and because you are giving significant authority to your "agent" over your matters, it is **essential** that you consult an attorney in your state to properly complete and validate any legal POA forms.*

Principal (Your Info):

Name: _____

Address: _____

Phone: _____

Agent (Person You Grant POA To):

Name: _____

Relationship: _____

Phone: _____

Authority Granted:

- ☐ Financial matters
- ☐ Medical decisions
- ☐ Legal representation
- ☐ Real estate transactions
- ☐ Other: _____

Effective Date:

- ☐ Immediately
- ☐ Only upon incapacity (springing POA)
- ☐ Specific time frame: _____

HEALTH CARE PROXY TEMPLATE

A health care proxy allows you to appoint someone you trust to make medical decisions on your behalf if you're unable to do so. Many states Departments of Health provide free, downloadable forms on their websites, and most hospitals or medical professionals can supply standard templates as well. While it's possible to complete a health care proxy on your own, it's a good idea to review it with a legal or medical professional to ensure your wishes are clearly documented and the form complies with your state's requirements.

1. I,_____ , hereby appoint (name, home address and phone number) as my health care agent to make any and all health care decisions for me, except to the extent that I state otherwise. This proxy shall take effect when and if I become unable to make my own health care decisions.

2. Optional: Alternate Agent. If the person I appoint is unable, unwilling or unavailable to act as my health care agent, I hereby appoint: (name, home address and telephone number) as my health care agent to make any and all health care decisions for me, except to the extent that I state otherwise.

3. Unless I revoke it or state an expiration date or circumstances under which it will expire, this proxy shall remain in effect indefinitely. (Optional: If you want this proxy to expire, state the date or conditions here.) This proxy shall expire (specify date or conditions):

4. Optional: I direct my health care agent to make health care decisions according to my wishes and limitations, as he or she knows or as stated below.

    (If you want to limit your agent's authority to make health care decisions for you or to give specific instructions, you may state your wishes or limitations here.)

5. I direct my health care agent to make health care decisions in accordance with the following limitations and/or instructions (attach additional pages as necessary).

    In order for your agent to make health care decisions for you about artificial nutrition and hydration (nourishment and water provided by feeding tube and intravenous line), your agent must reasonably know your wishes. You can either tell your agent what your wishes are or include them in this section.

6. Optional: Organ and/or Tissue Donation. I hereby make an anatomical gift, to be effective upon my death, of: Any needed organs and/or tissues or the following organs and/or tissues

    Limitations If you do not state your wishes or instructions about organ and/or tissue donation on this form, it will not be taken to mean that you do not wish to make a donation or prevent a person, who is otherwise authorized by law, to consent to a donation on your behalf.

7. Statement by Witnesses: (Witnesses must be 18 years of age or older and cannot be the health care agent or alternate.)

HOME INVENTORY WORKSHEET

Use this worksheet to list, photograph, and document your belongings for renters or homeowners insurance. Walk through your home, room by room, with this worksheet and your phone. Take pictures of all your belongings as you write down a description on the worksheet. Take the time to locate receipts and keep a digital copy of those as well with the photos, as this will take a huge burden off your back at claim time. Keep a copy in a safe place (cloud drive, external hard drive, or printed copy stored offsite). Update the inventory at least once a year or after major purchases.

Room/ Location	Item Description	Brand/ Model/ Serial Number	Purchase Date	Purchase Amount/ Estimated Value	Photo (Y/N)	Receipt (Y/N)

CHAPTER 7 APPENDIX:

WORK AND CAREER FINANCIAL FIRST AID KIT

SALARY/RAISE REQUEST PREP LIST

- Have a clear idea of the job title and what would be your primary duties

- Note any responsibilities you've taken on beyond your job description

- Highlight major accomplishments (projects, milestones, improvements)

- Quantify your impact when possible (e.g., "increased sales by 15%," "saved the company $10,000")

- List skills you've gained or certifications you've earned

- Include any training or professional development completed

- Note how your work has helped your team, department, or company succeed

- Identify any problems you've solved or efficiencies you've created

- Research what others in your position make (use sites like Glassdoor, PayScale, or industry reports)

- Know the competitive salary range for your role and location

- Identify when your last raise or review occurred

- Mention recent positive feedback, performance reviews, or promotions

- Decide what salary (dollar amount) or raise (percentage or dollar amount) you're asking for

- Be realistic, based on your research and value

- Write out your pitch and practice saying it out loud

- Role-play with a trusted friend or mentor

- Prepare to answer questions or objections confidently - Know Your Worth!

TWO-WEEK NOTICE TEMPLATE

Giving a two-week notice is a professional courtesy that shows respect for your employer and helps preserve positive relationships. It allows time for the company to prepare for your departure, begin the hiring process, and transition your responsibilities smoothly. Leaving on good terms can also protect your reputation and lead to strong references in the future.

[Manager's Name]
[Company Name]
[Company Address]

Dear [Manager's Name],

I am writing to formally resign from my position as [Your Job Title] at [Company Name], effective two weeks from today. My last working day will be [Last Working Day, typically two weeks from the date above].

This was not an easy decision, as I have appreciated the opportunity to be part of your team. I am grateful for the experience and support I've received during my time here.

I will do my best to ensure a smooth transition, including training a replacement or wrapping up ongoing responsibilities as needed.

Thank you again for the opportunity. I wish you and the team continued success.

Sincerely,
[Your Name]

CHAPTER 8 APPENDIX:

SCAMS AND FRAUD FINANCIAL FIRST AID KIT

FRAUD ALERT CHECKLIST

If you suspect you've been targeted by a scam, taking quick and decisive action is critical. This checklist walks you through the immediate steps to protect your identity, limit damage, and report the fraud to the appropriate authorities. Keep it handy to be better prepared to respond swiftly and safeguard your financial health. Acting quickly is crucial to minimize damage.

1. **Cease All Contact** with the scammer or suspicious party and quickly jot down notes to document everything you remember as soon as possible.

2. **Freeze Your Credit and File a Fraud Alert** with the three bureaus:
   o   Equifax: 800-349-9960
   o   Experian: 888-397-3742
   o   TransUnion: 888-909-8872

3. **Report the Fraud** to:
   o   FTC: ReportFraud.ftc.gov
   o   Internet Crime Complaint Center (IC3): www.ic3.gov
   o   Local police or consumer protection agency
   o   IRS (if tax-related fraud)

4. **Contact Your Bank or Credit Card Company** to stop or reverse charges.

5. **Update Passwords and Enable Two-Factor Authentication.**

6. **Check Your Credit Reports** for unauthorized activity and continue to do so for at least the next two years.

7. **Alert Friends/Contacts** if the scam involved your email or social media.

FRAUD FILTER CHECKLIST: HOW TO SPOT A SCAM BEFORE IT'S TOO LATE

Use this checklist when you receive a suspicious message, call, or email. If you check two or more boxes, proceed with extreme caution. Scammers use emotion and urgency to override your logic. Take a breath, verify the facts, and never be afraid to say, "I'll call you back."

Communication Style Red Flags:

- The message feels urgent or creates panic ("Act now!" "Your account will be closed!")

- The caller or sender pressures you to stay on the line or respond right away

- You're asked to keep the situation a secret or not tell anyone

- You're contacted out of the blue by someone claiming to be from the government, tech support, or a loved one in trouble

Money & Payment Requests:

- They ask for payment via gift cards, wire transfers, cryptocurrency, or cash apps

- They want you to "verify your identity" by having you give your Social Security number, bank account, or login credentials

- You're told you've won money but you have to pay a fee to claim it

- You're asked to download an app or click a link to "resolve an issue"

Suspicious Email/Message Details:

- The email address or phone number looks odd or unfamiliar

- There are misspellings, bad grammar, or weird formatting

- The message includes a generic greeting like "Dear Customer" or "Hello Friend"

- Hyperlinks don't match the real website (hover over them but don't click to preview the true URL)

Technology Red Flags:

- The caller sounds "off," robotic, or suspiciously like a loved one

- You've seen similar scam alerts online (search the phone number, message, or email subject)

- The message includes a deepfake video or AI-generated voice and claims to be urgent or secret

What to Do Instead:

- Hang up or delete the message - don't engage

- Call the person, company, or agency back using a trusted number

- Report scams to the FTC at reportfraud.ftc.gov

- Freeze your credit if personal data was compromised

- Educate friends and family, **especially seniors**, on scam red flags

INVESTMENT RED FLAG WORKSHEET

Red Flag	Description
Unrealistic Returns	Promises of "guaranteed" high profits
Urgency or Pressure to Act Fast	Limited-time offers or pressure to commit now
Lack of Transparency	Vague info on how money is used or who is involved
Unregistered or Unlicensed	Individual or product not listed with SEC or FINRA
No Physical Address or Website	Hard to verify contact or company legitimacy
Secrecy Clauses	Told to keep investment "confidential"

EVERYDAY PRACTICES THAT MAKE CYBER SENSE

In today's digital world, scammers and hackers are always looking for opportunities, but you don't have to make it easy for them. These simple, everyday practices can go a long way in keeping your personal, financial, and professional data safe.

- Use strong, unique passwords for all accounts.

- Never reuse the same password across multiple sites.

- Consider using a password manager to securely store login details.

- Never click on suspicious links or open attachments from unknown senders.

- Verify the identity of anyone asking for money, gift cards, or personal information - especially through email, text, or social media.

- Always log out of accounts on shared or public computers.

- Avoid entering sensitive information over public Wi-Fi - use a VPN if necessary.

- Enable multi-factor authentication (MFA) on all accounts that offer it.

- Keep your computer, phone, and antivirus software up to date.

- Regularly check your bank and credit accounts for suspicious activity.

- Back up important files regularly in case of ransomware or hacking.

- Use privacy settings on social media to limit what strangers can see.

- Avoid oversharing personal information (like birthdates, travel plans, or family details) online.

- Be cautious with online quizzes, surveys, and contests - they may harvest data.

- Confirm websites are secure (look for "https") before entering payment or login info.

- Report phishing emails, scam texts, and suspicious websites immediately.

- Never respond to urgent or threatening messages asking for immediate action - scammers often create false urgency.

- Trust your instincts - if something feels off, pause and double-check.

CHAPTER 9 APPENDIX:

RELATIONSHIP AND EMOTIONAL FINANCIAL FIRST AID KIT

MONEY TALK CONVERSATION GUIDE

Talking about money doesn't have to be uncomfortable. In fact, it can be one of the most powerful ways to build trust and shared goals in any relationship. The key is to create a safe space where both people can speak openly and listen with respect. This guide offers conversation starters, planning prompts, and ongoing topics to help couples, partners, or roommates communicate clearly and avoid misunderstandings. **Schedule money talks during calm, neutral times and not during arguments or after a big spending event.** *With the right timing, tone, and mindset, these discussions can strengthen both your finances and your relationship.*

Start With:

- "What does financial security look like to you?"

- "What were money habits like in your family growing up?"

- "How do you feel about debt and credit cards?"

Planning Together:

- "What are our top 3 financial goals this year?"

- "How will we handle unexpected expenses?"

- "Should we have a shared budget or keep finances separate?"

Ongoing Topics:

- Monthly budget review

- Tracking shared expenses

- Setting savings targets

- Planning for large purchases

Ground Rules for the Conversation:

- Listen without judgment

- Be honest about financial fears

- Use "I" statements (e.g., "I feel stressed when...")

- Agree on a follow-up date

JOINT EXPENSE AGREEMENT FORM

Use this form to define financial responsibilities in shared living or partnership

Names of Parties:

- Person A: _____

- Person B: _____

Start Date: _____

End/Review Date (if any): _____

Expense Category	Notes (Who pays what % or $)
Rent/Mortgage	
Utilities (Gas, Water, Electric)	
Internet & Subscriptions	
Groceries	
Dining Out	
Transportation	
Childcare/Pet Expenses	
Household Supplies	
Other	
Signature of Agreement:	
Person A: _____	Person B: _____
Date: _____	Date: _____

FAMILY BOUNDARIES & BUDGET AGREEMENT TEMPLATE

Use this agreement to outline expectations when offering financial support to adult children or family members. It's not a legal document but meant to encourage open communication while helping set clear financial expectations and boundaries as well as accountability.

Agreement Between:

Support Provider (Name): _____

Recipient (Name): _____

Date: _____

Type of Financial Support:

(✓ Check all that apply)

☐ Rent/Housing Assistance

☐ Utilities

☐ Groceries

☐ Car Payment

☐ Credit Card/Loan Payment

☐ Tuition or Education Costs

☐ Emergency Support

☐ Other: _____

Duration of Support:

This support will be provided:

☐ One time only

☐   Monthly for _____ months (Start date: _____ / End date: _____)

☐   Until the following conditions are met:

Maximum Support Amount:

I/we agree to provide up to: $ _____ per month / one-time.

Funds will be:

☐   Given directly to the recipient

☐   Paid directly to the landlord/vendor/bill collector

Expectations of the Recipient:

(✓ Check all that apply or write your own)

☐   Create and share a monthly budget

☐   Actively seek employment or increase income

☐   Cut back on non-essential spending (e.g., dining out, shopping)

☐   Participate in financial coaching or credit counseling

☐   Provide monthly progress updates

☐   Attend a family meeting/check-in every _____ weeks

☐   Other: _____

Boundaries to Protect Our Relationship:

To preserve trust and avoid resentment, we agree:

•   to communicate openly and respectfully

•   that this agreement does not create long-term financial dependence

•   that failure to meet agreed-upon expectations may result in discontinued support

•   that future requests may require a new written agreement

Signatures:

Support Provider Signature: _____

Date: _____

Recipient Signature: _____

Date: _____

ADDITIONAL RESOURCES:

For more tools, worksheets, and updates, visit our website at www.dollarsandsensepublishing.com. Stay connected with us on Facebook, Instagram, Twitter and TikTok and continue learning as you build a brighter financial future.

WHO IS DOLLARS AND SENSE PUBLISHING?

We are a group of friends, all professionals in various fields, passionate about making financial and common sense matters simple to understand. With engaging posts and informative books, we want to better the lives of our followers and make a positive difference in the world.

We are on a mission to demystify the world of personal finance. In a world where common sense financial literacy is often overlooked in traditional education, we believe that everyone deserves access to clear, practical advice that can be applied to everyday life.

Our team of experienced professionals are dedicated to creating straightforward, actionable financial guides for banking, insurance, tax planning, cybersecurity and beyond. With a focus on empowering our readers to make informed financial decisions, we are committed to delivering content that is not only informative but also inspiring.

At Dollars and Sense Publishing, we're here to help you navigate your financial journey with confidence and clarity... starting today!

BRING FINANCIAL FIRST AID TO YOUR GROUP!

Interested in hosting a financial wellness talk, book discussion, or Q&A session based on Financial First Aid: A Dollars and Sense Guide to Avoiding and Fixing Costly Money Mistakes? Our team at Dollars and Sense Publishing offers practical, engaging presentations that focus on real-life money challenges, such as debt, overspending, emotional spending, and credit pitfalls, and how to fix them.

Whether you're a school, nonprofit, workplace, or community group looking to empower others with relatable, no-nonsense financial guidance, we tailor our sessions to meet your audience's needs. We break down financial concepts in a way that's easy to understand and even easier to apply.

Email us at dollarsandsensepub@gmail.com to schedule a session. We'll work with you to create an event that's insightful, encouraging, and packed with real-world strategies your group can use right away.

www.ingramcontent.com/pod-product-compliance
Lightning Source LLC
Chambersburg PA
CBHW070913130626
46555CB00001B/112